Minority Leadership in Community Colleges;
What Community College Boards, Legislators,
and Community Citizens Need to Know

Who's Leading at Your Community College?

by

Evangeline Smith

CORINNE DICKEY, Ph.D., Faculty Mentor and Chair

JERRY HALVERSON, Ph.D., Committee Member

CHERYL KNIGHT, Ph.D., Committee Member

Barbara Butts Williams, Ph.D., Dean, School of Education

A Dissertation Presented in Partial Fulfillment

Of the Requirements for the Degree

Doctor of Philosophy

Capella University

November 2011

Order this book online at www.trafford.com
or email orders@trafford.com

Most Trafford titles are also available at major online book retailers.

Print information available on the last page.

ISBN: 978-1-4907-5817-6 (sc)
ISBN: 978-1-4907-5816-9 (e)

Trafford rev. 10/28/2015

 www.trafford.com
North America & international
toll-free: 1 888 232 4444 (USA & Canada)
fax: 812 355 4082

Abstract

Community colleges in America, through organizations such as The American Association of Community Colleges (AACC) and the American Council on Education, have led the way by researching best practices and offering recommendations to improve the community college purpose and the role of the presidents and leaders. Recently, the AACC and others have noted that a leadership crisis is eminent because retirement for baby boomers is approaching and community colleges may not be prepared. Dr. Lopez-Molina (2008) conducted a research study that examined how three colleges prepared future leaders. The result of her research study revealed that even though college leaders (presidents) thought that they were developing future leaders their subordinates disagreed. This current study expanded Lopez-Molina's study of three community colleges in three different states by examining how eight community colleges in North Carolina are identifying and preparing future leaders and also determined if their demographic service area and student enrollment were reflected in their leadership teams. This research study determined that eight selected community colleges trained and prepared future leaders through national, state, and local staff development workshops, but not specifically through succession planning for leadership positions. This research study also revealed that upper-level leaders understood what succession planning and succession leadership implied, but noted that national, state, and local training were sufficient for preparing future leaders. Conversely, subordinates in this research study did not have a clear meaning of succession planning for leadership positions and desired that upper-level leaders would identify, train, and choose future leaders from among their existing ranks of leaders at these eight community colleges.

Dedication

his dissertation is dedicated to my husband, Charles E. Smith, who, even though he suffered from sickness and critical illness, strengthened me and encouraged me to endure to the end. I thank you my friend, my support, my hero. God bless you.

Acknowledgements

To Dr. Corinne Dickey, who personifies the true meaning of "angels among us," mentored me from the unchartered beginning to the glorious end. Dr. Dickey, you have no idea that through your mentoring I have gained perseverance that defeated all odds that I would reach this plateau. I thank you for keeping the light burning so I could see. Also, special thanks go to Dr. Jerry Halverson and Dr. Cheryl Knight who served as my committee members and gave me inspiring suggestions and support throughout this dissertation process.

I would like to acknowledge William and Jessie Mae Stephens Ferguson, my parents, who instilled in me hope, faith, and love. To my children, Charlene Arrington, Abby Haywood, and William Cedric Smith, I thank you for supporting me as I walked through the valley of trials and tribulations. I love you and I am deeply grateful for having you to protect my heart. To my beautiful grandchildren, Jessika, Ammber, Andre, and Chay, I love you.

Special thanks to Dr. Delores Parker, Vice President of the North Carolina Community College System, and Dr. Donald Cameron, President of Guilford Technical Community college, who shared their insights and knowledge and encouraged me to embark on this research journey.

Finally, I would like to acknowledge Capella University's support staff that never let me down when I called or needed help during my educational journey. You are great professionals!

Contents

List of Tables

List of Figures

CHAPTER I. INTRODUCTION

Introduction: North Carolina Community Colleges

The North Carolina Community College System (NCCS) consists of 58 community colleges located in both rural and urban areas throughout North Carolina, governed by a system president. Existing as the third largest community college system in the nation, approximately 750,000 students attend community colleges throughout the state. The North Carolina Community College System's mission is to provide educational opportunities for its citizenry throughout the 100 counties in the state. One of its main objectives is to provide job-training opportunities for learners so that businesses and industries can hire from a qualified workforce. The job training opportunities offered by the community colleges prepare and train learners to be able to compete in a global workforce.

Another aim of the North Carolina Community College System is to provide higher educational learning alternatives by offering programs that yield certificates, diplomas, and associate degrees for its learners. The North Carolina Community College System promotes economic and community development by collaborating with local businesses and industries throughout the state to train and prepare a competent workforce.

To endorse post-secondary education, The North Carolina Community College System offers transfer programs and pre-baccalaureate programs with the University of North Carolina System as well as private colleges and universities. Students who complete their post-secondary education are equipped to compete in the higher educational arena.

Most importantly, the North Carolina Community College System serves a multicultural population to acknowledge the value of diversity and strengthen the success of individuals who enroll in the community colleges. Community college students are provided pathways to ensure success in a range of studies from basic skills and literacy to occupational and post-secondary education.

When President Lancaster retired from the North Carolina Community College System office in 2007, he perceived that the community college system would be facing massive retirements and possible leadership gaps within some of the system's institutions. He noted that 59 presidents, 54 senior administrators, 48 curriculum faculty and 48 staff members were eligible for retirement. He concluded that the North Carolina Community College System would need trained and qualified leaders to replace potential retirees between 2010 and 2014.

President Lancaster made it clear that future leadership and succession needs and planning for the North Carolina Community College System must be clearly understood and seriously considered by the leaders in the system's state office. He also specified that as enrollment increases, expanding new programs and turnover of employees from presidents to custodians will contribute to the need for the North Carolina Community College System office leaders to consider succession planning in the near future (Lancaster, 2007). Still, more than two years after President Lancaster stated his concerns, there are no leadership development and/or succession planning opportunities in existence through the NCCC system office.

Introduction to the Problem

According to O'Banion (2006), "Community colleges are facing a major crisis in leadership" (p. 46). He went on to say, "We do not have programs to prepare enough new doctoral students to become future presidents, vice presidents and program leaders that we need. Unless something is done to address this situation, we are going to be in grave trouble" (p. 47). O'Banion's (2006) study revealed not only that there may be a potential leadership crisis, but that higher level educational institutions are not offering programs that prepare learners to become higher level leaders in higher education.

Duree (2008) conducted a study on the retirement status of community college presidents and discovered that "of 415 community college presidents--representing 38.2

percent of the national total---79 percent will retire by 2012, and 84 percent by 2016"
(p. 1). Duree's (2008) study is supported by The American Association of Community
Colleges (2006) which concluded that baby boomers will be retiring and could possibly
create a shortage of qualified leaders in community college systems. Because of the
leadership crisis noted by O'Banion (2006), Duree (2008), and The American Association
of Community Colleges (2006), this current project's focus was to research eight
selected community colleges in North Carolina and determine their readiness to meet
this impending leadership crisis. In particular, this study investigated such measures as
succession planning, identifying and preparing future leaders, with specificity toward
determining if minorities were given a chance to participate in succession planning for
higher level leadership positions.

Background of the Study

Research studies have shown that community colleges are facing a potential
leadership crisis because of the need to replace baby boomers who are reaching
retirement age (Cohen, 2002; Jamilah, 2006; Wolverton, Gmelch, Wolverton, & Sarros
1999). Moreover, Duree's (2008) study documented that the number of community
college leadership program graduates decreased by 78% from 1983 to 1997. Duree (2008)
warned in his research that

> If you think about that time period, those would be the people who would really
> be in the chute to take the place of those who were retiring. So actually, not only
> is there the anticipated exodus going out the door, but there also is a shortage of
> qualified candidates coming in. (p. 1)

Administrators in community colleges often search outside the hiring community
college for leaders, instead of searching from within their ranks for administrative
possibilities. Local administrators are skillful and their duties include building teaching
and learning relationships with learners, coordinating community programs, mentoring
peers, and establishing educational partnerships with community businesses at large.

Existing leaders become diversified in adapting and utilizing leadership strategies to develop and enhance community college programs. Most middle-level leaders report to deans, provosts, vice-presidents, and presidents. Perhaps some of these individuals are prepared as middle-level leaders able to move into upper level positions currently held by baby boomers nearing retirement.

Since the creation of the first community college, Joliet Junior College in 1901 in Joliet, Illinois, the community college's mission, vision, and leadership role evolves and governs through controversy. Pedersen (1997) perceived,

> When an institution's purposes are many and poorly integrated, and incompletely understood, conflict arises among those it charges with carrying out these purposes. Under such conditions, an action taken by one member of the organization to further the institution's mission and purpose will almost certainly be challenged by another as directly threatening some fundamental institutional value. (p. 499)

The leadership role in community colleges affects and shapes their mission, vision, goals, and cultural, economical, and political agendas. Lopez-Molina (2008) stated, "The changing nature of the social, racial/ethnic, economic, and political agendas of America continues to redefine the role of community colleges in America" (p. 12). If the role of a community college is directed by social, racial/ethnic, economic and political agendas, should not the leadership role, mission, and vision, be redefined and shaped to reflect its racial/ethnic, economic, and political populations as well?

Higher education demands research and the community college, as a higher education institution, currently has an opportunity as well as an obligation to employ succession planning research for succession leadership. Succession planning research for succession leadership will help identify strengths, weaknesses, and leadership gaps in community colleges' leadership pools. Succession planning research may also identify minorities who may be interested in higher educational leadership positions within the community college system for community college leaders who desire to enhance diversity leadership opportunities.

This current research was a replication of the Lopez-Molina (2008) study and examined eight selected North Carolina community colleges to identify individuals who might assist community college presidents in determining how the departure of retiring baby boomers will impact and create a leadership crisis in those selected North Carolina community colleges.

Statement of the Problem

Research showed that community college leaders have known about the plausible leadership crisis since at least 2001 (Amey & VanDerlinden, 2006; Duree, 2008; Leubsdorf, 2006; O'Banion, 2006). Leubsdorf (2006) declares, "An estimated 6,000 jobs in postsecondary-education administration will have to be filled annually between 2004 and 2014" (p. 1). As some researchers have noted, mid-level managers may not be prepared to replace upper-level management positions because universities have not offered programs that prepare as many doctoral candidates as are needed to replace upper-level positions (American Association of Community Colleges, [AACC], 2002; Duree, 2008; O'Banion, 2006; Park, 2006).

Purpose of the Study

The purpose of this study was to investigate if eight selected North Carolina community colleges were preparing to meet the impending leadership crisis in higher-level leadership positions as forecasted by The American Association of Community Colleges and others. This current research sought to determine if succession planning is employed for succession leadership as an instrument to identify potential leaders at the eight selected community colleges. This current study specifically investigated if minorities at these selected North Carolina community colleges had opportunities to participate in leadership development programs.

Rationale

The literature review revealed that

Higher education has historically been slow to adopt many corporate management processes. Succession planning is an especially difficult concept to apply in academia due to dramatic cultural differences between the boardroom and the campus. Colleges and universities often have complex and sometimes bureaucratic procedures for hiring compared with many business corporations. (Clunies, 2004)

Clunies (2004) revealed, "As reported by others, there is little new research on succession planning in recent years. And there is an ongoing dearth of writing about succession planning as applied in higher education." (p. 1) If educational institutions have not studied succession planning, how do they know whether it will work in higher education institutions?

Within the body of recent literature, Carlson (2007) and Lopez-Molina (2008) conducted a study about succession planning in community colleges. Carlson's (2007) study revealed that "However, many community colleges do not have succession-leadership plans or leadership- development programs available to their employees. Although leadership-development programs have been studied at community colleges, research is needed to determine what constitutes an effective program" (p.138).

Lopez-Molina (2008) advocated that district community colleges conduct succession planning research to determine if community colleges are implementing leadership development programs both to identify potential leaders and thwart the impeding leadership exodus. Lopez-Molina (2008) stated, "It is recommended this study be replicated in other community colleges districts to determine if other community college districts are identifying and preparing future leaders" (p. 6). She went on to say that future researchers should "expand the study to include more colleges" (p. 98).

Therefore, the rationale for this study was warranted. This research study replicated Lopez-Molina's (2008) study and collected data from eight selected North Carolina Community college presidents, administrators, and faculty. The study raised awareness as it determined leadership succession plans implemented to identify the next tier of leaders necessary as baby boomers retire. This current research determined if employees express an interest in higher-level positions in community colleges and will identify potential future leaders. Finally, this current research investigated if selected North Carolina community colleges are prepared to face an impending leadership crisis with an emphasis on the role of minority leaders as potential high-level leaders in community colleges.

Research Questions

Because of the impending leadership crisis facing community colleges and the recommendation to expand the research on succession planning in community college districts, the following questions for this research study were adapted and modified from Lopez-Molina's (2008) study as follows:

1. To what extent are selected community colleges in North Carolina preparing future leaders?
2. How are leadership development programs in North Carolina's selected community colleges related to succession planning for employees?
3. How do succession planning strategies include considerations for social, economic and political/cultural nuances for developing leaders in selected North Carolina community colleges?
4. How do research findings show parallels and/or patterns as they are compared to research findings of Lopez-Molina (2008) and Carlson (2007)?

Significance of the Study

The North Carolina Community College System is the third largest in the United States and is comprised of 58 community colleges serving 100 counties. Numerous continuing education leaders are a fundamental part of the administration tiers in community colleges. The review of the literature reiterated the fact that impending retirement of current community college leaders will create a crisis in community college leadership positions within 2004 to 2014 and that there will soon be a massive shortage of qualified higher education leaders (Leubsdorf, 2006; O'Banion, 2006, 2007; Outcalt, 2002; Viniar, 2006).

The review of the literature also revealed that higher education institutions cannot prepare doctoral candidates to fulfill these much-needed administrative positions in higher education (AACC, 2002). According to Lopez-Molina (2008) and others, it is necessary to conduct research that will identify potential leaders and that higher educational institutions move forward to implement leadership development programs. She stated, "In anticipation of and response to the projected major exodus of current leadership in higher education institutions, it is important that colleges and universities consider collaborative efforts through an accreditation of leadership development programs" (p. 6). This current research study expanded upon Lopez-Molina's (2008) study and included more colleges and identified those colleges that have existing leadership developmental programs in eight selected North Carolina community colleges. The responsibility of this kind of leadership development/succession research, in the words of Lopez-Molina (2008), will:

> ...add to the concept of a national model of community college leadership development (Gould, 2007a, 3007b). The notion of a national model for leadership development through succession planning may lead the institution to further elaborate; providing educational pathways for leadership development from the associate's degree through the articulation with four-year through graduate studies. (p. 6)

Definitions of Terms

The following terms with applied meaning were recognized in this research:

Acculturation. Defined as changes in cultural attitudes, values, and behaviors that result from sustained contact between two or more distinct cultures (Berry, 1980).

Cultural Cognizance. Being aware, cognizant, observant and conscious of similarities and differences among cultural groups (National Center for Cultural Competence, (2009).

Cultural Competency. Having the capacity to function effectively cross-culturally through integration of human behavior that includes thoughts, communications, actions, customs, beliefs, values and institutions of a racial, ethnic, religious or social group (National Center for Cultural Competence, (2009).

Cultural Intelligence. A person's capacity to adapt effectively to new cultural settings or contexts based on multiple facets including cognitive, motivational, and behavioral features (Molinsky, 2007).

Cultural Nuances. A subtle distinction or variation of social, behavioral, and traditional norms specific to a particular group, community, race/Ethnicity/culture (Mendez-Morse, 2004; Baker, 1999).

Culture. Sum total of ways of living including behavioral norms, language, communication style, patterns of thinking, and beliefs and values (National Center for Cultural Competence, 2009).

Human Resource Leader. A leader who understands that organizations need people for their energy, effort and talent (Bolman & Deal, 2003).

Institutional Climate. The commonly shared workplace environment conducive to the nurturing of the institutional culture (Bolman & Deal, 2003).

Institutional Culture. Standards that include, but not limited to, norms, values, beliefs, and behaviors shared and expressed by decision-makers of an institution (Bolman & Deal, 2003; Gardner, 1990; Gould & Caldwell, 1998; Ramsden, 2000).

Leadership. "Leadership is the process of persuasion or example by which an individual (or leadership team) induces a group to pursue objectives held by the leader or shared by the leader and his or her followers" (Gardner, 1990).

Leadership Development. The development of the leader through a process; the focus on the building and expanding on the knowledge, skills, and abilities for effective leadership with desired outcomes and expectations (Cashman, 1998; Gardner, 1990; Ramsden, 2000).

Political leader. A leader who understands that organizational change and effectiveness depend on managers' political understanding and skills (Bolman & Deal, 2003).

Structural leader. A leader who understands that "organizations divide work by creating a variety of specialized roles, functions, and units" (Bolman & Deal, 2003).

Succession planning. The process of identifying and preparing a suitable employee for a position or replacement of an employee in a different role within the organization or institution through job rotation, training and mentoring (American Heritage Dictionary of the English Language (2009).

Symbolic leader. A leader who understands "the culture, symbols, myths and stories of the organization and, gives direction in the midst of chaos" (Bolman & Deal, 2003).

Assumptions and Limitations

Newman and Benz (1998) stated, "All research in education stands on basic underlying assumptions" (p. 8). For research to be scientific there must be suppositions and hypotheses.

The authors stated,

> Science is both positivistic and naturalistic in its assumptions. Two fundamental epistemological requirements are made of the researcher: one must clearly and openly acknowledge one's assumptions about what counts as known and maintain consistency in those assumptions and the methods that derive from them. To us, this is what makes the research scientific (p. 16).

It is important to understand in research that "limitations to validity exist" (Newman & Benz, 1998, p. 68) and that these limitations must be stated in the research. By stating assumptions and limitations the researcher identifies potential implied biases. Therefore, limitations and assumptions for this research study are stated below.

Assumptions

1. Participants in this research study participated freely, ethically, and honestly.
2. Leadership development programs are available for staff and faculty to aspire to higher educational leadership positions.
3. Participants understood what was being asked in the research instruments.
4. Selected North Carolina institutions currently have a succession plan.
5. Selected North Carolina institutions are preparing future leaders who are representative of the student population

Limitations

1. Due to the nature of this research, it must be noted that this researcher may or may not have been biased.
2. Participants may or may not have understood succession planning or succession leadership.
3. Participants may or may not trusted the validity of securing the data and may or may not answered truthfully with regard to revealing disparity in hiring practices by their institutions.
4. Selected institutions in North Carolina may have been reticent in providing demographic data related to students and employees.
5. This research study was conducted on selected community colleges in North Carolina and may not be representative of community colleges in general.

Theoretical Framework

Philosophical concepts are foundations for theoretical frameworks (Senge, 1990). To reveal a philosophy or concept, one has to present the originator of the concept or philosophy and make explicit how the concept contributes to the values, mission, and vision of the research or system (Lynham, 2002). This current research was guided by theoretical frameworks in literature on leadership, leadership theories, leadership styles, succession leadership and succession planning, and implications for future leaders in community colleges. In addition, this study compared and contrasted succession plans and leadership development practices in selected North Carolina community colleges. Transformational leadership and servant leader were the two main leadership theories that were discussed as they are relative for future leaders to serve their stakeholders (Bolman & Deal 2003; Greenleaf, 1997; Lopez-Molina, 2008; Polleys, 2002). In addition, to illustrate how future community college leaders can implement change in community colleges, Bolman and Deal's (2003) four leadership types were discussed.

Servant Leadership

Polleys (2002) described the nature of a servant leader as "one who puts serving others, including employees, customers, and community as the number one priority" (para. 9).

She went on to include Greenleaf's (1997) definition of servant leader as:

> The servant leader is servant first. It begins with the natural feeling
> that one wants to serve, to serve first. Then conscious choice brings one
> to aspire to lead ... [servant leadership] manifests itself in the care
> taken to make sure that other people's highest priority needs are being
> served. The best test, and difficult to administer, is: Do those served
> grow as persons? Do they, while being served, become healthier, wiser,
> freer, more autonomous, more likely themselves to become servants? And what
> is the effect on the least privileged in society; will they benefit, or, at
> least, not be further deprived? (para.10)

Transformational Leadership

Transformational leadership is leadership that motivates and inspires followers. The expectation of transformational leadership is that leaders, followers, and policies are parts of complete transformation occurring in organizations (Avolio & Bass, 2002; Bolman & Deal, 2003; Story, 2004).

Review of the literature demonstrated that future leaders must be prepared to transform community colleges and serve their "constituencies" (Lopez-Molina, 2008). Research demonstrated that not only do future leaders have to serve their constituencies and transform their organization, as noted by Lopez-Molina (2008), but they also have to demonstrate an understanding of organizational culture, politics, human resources, and structural components, when transforming and serving constituencies in organizations (Bolman & Deal, 2003).

Bolman and Deal's Leadership Types

Bolman and Deal's (2003) four frames for reframing organizations were integrated within the literature review to demonstrate how future community college leaders can utilize the four frames theory to better serve and transform community colleges.

The first frame is the structural frame. Bolman and Deal (2003) defined a structural leader as one "who understands that organizations divide work by creating a variety of specialized roles, functions, and units" (p. 67). As it related to this current research, this illustrated that leadership development plans can create an opportunity for potential leaders to build leadership skills so potential leaders are prepared to function in various roles, and departments.

The second frame is the human resource frame. Bolman and Deal (2003) stated, "Human resource theorists typically advocate openness, mutuality, listening, coaching, participation, and empowerment. They view of the leader is as a facilitator and catalyst who motivates and empowers subordinates" (p. 354). Again, as related to this current research, this frame could promote succession planning that would empower subordinates by building leadership skills necessary for potential leaders to succeed.

The third leadership frame is the political frame. The political leader, as viewed by Bolman and Deal (2003), is a leader who "views organizations as living, screaming political arenas that host a complex web of individual and group interests" (p. 186). Community colleges operate under political influences, both internally and externally. Townsend and Twombley (2001) explained the political forces that influence the governance of community colleges:

Yet community colleges are buffered from direct interaction with their external environments to the extent that government policies and funding behaviors, collective agreements between management and labor, institutional structures such as governance committees, federal regulations, and the like separate societal and global actions such as a recession in Asia or a downturn in the North American forestry industry from the colleges. These external actions are mediated by others, and the colleges become subordinate to external players, reactors to others' actions. In reacting, colleges focus on internal mechanisms, internal politics, internal personalities, and members' personal preferences, unaware at times of the global forces acting upon their institutions or, indeed, experiencing government behaviors that themselves are responses to globalization. Not all colleges, however, are distanced or protected from their external environments; furthermore, colleges protected from some conditions, such as state economic recessions, are not protected from others, such as local demographic changes as a result of refugees and immigrants. (p. 78)

Distance and local political changes infiltrate the complexity of community colleges as well as global forces and technologies. Townsend and Twombly (2001) further stated:

Colleges are buffeted by external forces, including global forces such as changing global economies; the rise and expansion of new technologies; the demands of government for greater productivity and efficiency; the changing workplace, with its emphasis on global competitiveness; and the movement of recent immigrants and refugees from Asia, the former Soviet Union countries, and war torn Balkan countries to communities surrounding these colleges. In almost contradictory fashion, community colleges are both buffered and buffeted institutions, being simultaneously buffered from a global environment and buffeted by global forces. (p. 78)

The final leadership frame that Bolman and Deal (2003) defined is the symbolic leader. The symbolic leader "understands the culture, symbols, myths and stories of the organization and gives direction in the midst of chaos", according to Bolman and Deal

(2003, p. 23). These four leadership frames were integrated within the literature review as part of the theoretical framework on leadership, leadership styles and succession planning and leadership development in community colleges.

The literature review revealed very little research has been conducted in the area of succession planning in higher education, especially within community colleges. It appeared that community college leaders may lack interest in developing leaders from within their institutions and, consequently, their employees often may not know when higher-level leadership positions are available or how these leadership positions may be pursued.

Brown, Martinez, and Daniel (2008) noted, "higher education institutions have a lack of interest in developing administrative leadership; institutions have paid little systematic attention to developing their own leaders" (p. 1). Therefore, it behooves community colleges to change their leadership appointment practices by adopting leadership development programs and employ succession planning for succession leadership.

The research study conducted by Lopez-Molina (2008) found that "administrations at Institutions A, B, C are not aware to what extent their respective institution is preparing future leaders" (p. 93). In this current research study the overarching questions are: Are selected North Carolina community colleges aware of the impending leadership crisis? And secondly, are they preparing future leaders (including minorities) through succession planning for higher-level leadership positions?

As stated earlier, this study replicated Lopez-Molina's (2008) study and slightly modified the research questions and adapted them to the selected North Carolina community colleges in this study. This current research expanded from three community colleges in three different states studied in the Lopez-Molina (2008) study to eight selected community colleges in North Carolina. This current replication study accented constructive replication. Constructive replication according to Gall, Gall, and Borg (2003) "increases the validity of theoretical studies in education" (p. 146). These authors recommend replication studies and stated, "You should seriously consider replication and extending previous studies rather than trying to investigate a previously unsolved problem" (p. 147).

Nature of the Study

This current research study used the mixed methods design by combining both quantitative (surveys) and qualitative (interviews) research.

Creswell and Plano Clark (2008) stated,

Mixed method research is a research design with philosophical assumptions as well as methods of inquiry. As a methodology, it involves philosophical assumptions that guide the direction of the collection and analysis of data and the mixture of qualitative and quantitative approaches in many phases in the research process. As a method, it focuses on collecting, analyzing, and mixing both quantitative and qualitative data in a single study or series of studies. Its central premise is that the use of quantitative and qualitative approaches in combination provides a better understanding of research problems than either approach alone. (p. 5)

Creswell and Plano Clark (2007) further stated,

Methodological triangulation is the use of at least two methods, usually qualitative and quantitative, to address the same research problem. When a singular research method is inadequate, triangulation is used to ensure that the most comprehensive approach is taken to solve a research problem. (p. 152)

In this current research study the triangulation design was used to correlate, compare, and contrast survey results that were both quantitative (surveys) and qualitative (interviews) and identified links, patterns, and/or discovered provocative information. The quantitative data was collected through the use of a two-part survey (Appendix A) and the qualitative phase was interview questions (Appendix B). After the data were collected, they were studied, compared, analyzed, and, hopefully, provocative information was discovered that will be useful to community colleges and will enhance the body of literature regarding succession planning and leadership development.

Triangulation, as defined by Creswell and Plano Clark (2007) referred to the

...design used by multiple methods research, with offsetting or counteracting biases, in investigations of the same phenomenon in order to strengthen the validity of inquiry results. The core premise of triangulation as a design strategy is that all methods have inherent biases and limitations, so use of only one method to assess a given phenomenon will inevitably yield biased and limited results. However, when two or more methods that have offsetting biases are used to assess a given phenomenon and the results of these methods converge or corroborate one another, then the validity of inquiry findings is enhanced. (p. 123)

Organization of the Remainder of the Study

This research study consisted of five chapters. Chapter 2 was the Literature Review. The literature review included the following subjects: (a) how scholars grappled with the complexity of the definition of leadership from simple to complex, (b) the pathways of governance in community colleges and determined what characteristics future community college leaders should embrace to better serve their employers, students, and community at large, and (c) compared, correlated, reviewed, and contrasted leadership theories and how succession planning and mentoring can be employed within the culture of the community college to prepare potential leaders, including minorities. Chapter 3 discussed the methodology, Chapter 4 discussed data collection and analysis, and Chapter 5 reported the results, conclusions, and recommendations.

Chapter Summary

Wallin, Cameron, and Sharpies (2005) stated:

Good leadership makes colleges work. Good leadership supports faculty and teaching, values students and learning, and reaches out to the community. Good leadership looks to the future. A growing number of colleges and boards of trustees are looking for the future by embracing succession planning as the key to assuring college sustainability in an environment that requires global thinking, strategic planning and political savvy. Once confined to the corporate world or the family business, and limited to CEO, succession planning has assumed a prominent role in progressive and innovative community colleges concerned about leadership at all levels. These colleges, their leadership teams, and their governing boards view succession planning as targeted leadership development that promotes a culture of learning, growing, and collaboration within the institution. (p. 1)

The 58 community colleges in North Carolina are facing a massive retirement crisis within the next decade. As community colleges continue to grow and serve the demands of its population in an economic crisis, they must first address its leadership needs to direct the future success of its mission, goals, and objectives. Many of the community college presidents, administrators, and faculty who began their careers in the early 1960s and 1970s are nearing the end of their careers and potentially, upon retirement, will create a deficit in the ranks of qualified leaders in the middle- and upper-level management positions.

Now is the time for community colleges to assess and identify their next tier of potential leaders and develop succession plans and/or leadership development plans that will thwart the impending leadership crisis that is forecast by The American Association of Community Colleges and others. It is also time to identify if and/or how community colleges need to address the leadership crisis and to explore what preparations, if any, are being made to identify potential leaders.

The focus of this current research investigated if administrators at eight selected North Carolina community colleges were identifying and preparing their future leaders in an effort to respond proactively to the predicted leadership crisis within the next decade and discerned if minorities have equal opportunities to lead.

CHAPTER 2. LITERATURE REVIEW

Introduction

Higher education institutions are facing an impending leadership crisis as a result of baby boomers' projected retirement in the next decade. According to Betts, Urias, Chaves, and Betts (2009), this impending leadership crisis was first forecasted by Shults in 2001 and the American Association of Community Colleges in 2006. Betts et al. (2009) stated:

> Higher education provides extensive opportunities for individuals seeking career, career transition, and career advancement. The U. S. Bureau of Labor Statistics projects there are an estimated 6,000 jobs in higher education administration that will be needed to be filled annually through 2014 (Leubsdorf, 2006, p. A51). Additionally, national research by the American Association of Community colleges (AACE) (2001) and Fain (2008) reveals that 79% of current community college presidents will retire by 2012 and 84% will retire by 2016. (para. 1)

With these alarming statistics, community colleges governing boards and presidents have the wonderful opportunity to become change agents and thwart the impending leadership crisis. Lopez-Molina (2008) stated: "The nation's community colleges have the opportunities to develop strategies to begin institutionalizing effective leadership development program initiatives that foster the development of the future leaders and provide for effective succession planning" (p. 56).

Since the founding of Joliet Junior College in Illinois in 1901, the community college has proven to be a vital part of the growth in higher education and has impacted the lives of millions of Americans. Americans from all walks of life and socio-economic backgrounds rely on community colleges "open doors" policy to allow each student the opportunity to improve the quality of his or her life. Community colleges are at the heart of each community in which they are established. In 1997 Goodchild and Wechsler posed this question: "Why Were Junior Colleges Established in the First Place?" The answer to the question lies in the "civic" wishes of the community in which they were built. Goodchild and Wechsler (1997) answered their own question when they stated:

> The motivations of civic leaders in such cities as Temple, Texas, and Everett, Washington, were not ideological. They were not driven by a desire to extend the common school, or to democratize access, or to advance meritocratic notions of higher education. There objective was civic development, and they saw this goal being realized primarily through an aggressive program of institution building. (p. 205)

The literature review revealed that as the needs of people in communities change due to urbanization and industrialization, institutional building of community colleges progressed rapidly. Urbanization and industrialization had their impact on the growth of community colleges (Betts et al., 2009; Goodchild & Wechsler, 1997). The Morrill Act of 1862 and the GI Bill had the greatest impact on institutional building and student enrollment in higher education (Goodchild & Wechsler, 1997). The Morrill Act of 1862 stated:

> Each state which may take and claim the benefit of this act, to the endowment, support, and maintenance of at least one college where the leading objective shall be, branches of learning as are related to agriculture and the mechanic arts, in such manner as the legislatures of the States may respectively prescribe, in order to promote the liberal and practical education of the industrial classes in the several pursuits and professions in life. (Goodchild & Wechsler, 1998, p. 362)

By promoting educational programs that offer agriculture and mechanic arts learning, the legislation set forth by the Morrill Act of 1862 was the foundation of open door policy education which brought on the expansion of community colleges.

Lopez-Molina (2008) stated: "In addition, the Morrill Act withheld funding from states refusing to admit students to their colleges based on race which facilitated greater access to higher education for minorities" (AACC, 2007b; Lopez-Molina, 2008, p. 13).

The G.I. (General Issue) Bill passed in a time when America had experienced a recession period and was facing the impact of millions of veterans returning from the war. Greenberg (1997) stated: "After the fighting ended, in August 1945, the nation faced a massive demobilization of military personnel and a change from a wartime economy to one responsive to neglected civilian needs" (para. 6). Here again, the needs of the community impact the growth of higher education. Greenberg (1997) continued:

> Spurred by the G.I. bill, 7.8 million veterans took advantage of its educational benefits. About 2.2 million went to college, but millions more received high-school diplomas, vocational education, and on-the-job training. Colleges and universities -- then largely small, elite, white, and liberal arts institutions -- confronted unprecedented demands for enrollments, housing, and more work-oriented curricula in engineering and business. In 1940 about 1.5 million students were enrolled, and about 180,000 graduated with bachelor's degrees. Within a decade, enrollments had risen to 2.7 million, representing all races and religions, and graduates numbered more than 400,000. (para. 7)

Not only did the GI Bill revolutionize higher education, it also lessened discrimination against Jews and Catholics, but minority Americans, once again, were denied the rights to higher education. Greenberg (1997) explained:

> One vital caveat: In 1944 America was a racially segregated society, and while black veterans would make substantial headway in joining the middle class, many were unable to overcome numerous barriers to participation in higher education. Discrimination against Jews and Catholics in many colleges and universities, however, virtually disappeared under the GI Bill. Women were largely uninvolved, although an estimated 64,000 out of 350,000 female veterans did enroll in college. (para. 8)

The GI Bill was a major catalyst that launched enrollment of higher education in American colleges and universities. In summary, Greenberg (1997) stated:

> To say that the GI Bill of 1944 was transformative is an understatement. It was revolutionary. It is widely acknowledged to be one of the major tipping points in American history. Colleges and universities multiplied, especially in urban areas. The major shortage of a skilled work force was met with the education of tens of thousands of engineers, accountants, teachers, doctors, dentists, lawyers, and research scientists, who were followed into higher education by their children and grandchildren. Higher education was turned from a hope to an expectation irrespective of age, gender, or social class. Upward mobility became the hallmark of the higher-education enterprise. (para. 9)

Presidents in higher education, colleges and universities, are facing similar challenges today. Currently, unemployment rates are high and many Americans are searching for career changes and are looking for new goals and new opportunities. Other challenges are in the field of new scientific discoveries and technology. Carlson (2007) stated:

> At the same time the new millennium has brought new challenges and changes to higher education that includes technology, student population demographics, and financial access. Other trends include competition for funds and students, management efficiency, flexibility in teaching and delivery, and global networks for local institutions. Issues specifically related to the community colleges include funding reductions, student population growth, technology needs, community partnerships, efficiency, and accountability. (p. 23)

Community college presidents can be harbingers of new change, new innovation, and new leadership styles. They have opportunities to "lead" their community colleges rather than "manage" them to their next level of expansion. Community colleges can be expanded through new program development and leadership development programs for succession leadership. Lopez-Molina (2008) advocated, "It is critical institutions proactively address the succession planning needed in their hiring practices for the new leadership" (p. 17).

Due to demographic statistics of real and projected population growth in the United States (see Figures 1 and 2 below) which may lead to higher enrollees in community colleges, now is the time for community college presidents to launch a change through succession planning for succession leadership. Betts et al. (2009) reported:

In 2007, the US Census Bureau reported the US population reached 301.6 million people of which 34% or 102.5 million were minorities (Bernstein, 2008). According to population projections, minorities will increase from approximately one-third to over half of the US population reaching 54% in 2050, representing 235.7 million out of the total US population of 439 million (Bernstein & Edwards, 2008). Among all races, only White non-Hispanics are projected to lose population growth between 2008 and 2050 decreasing from 66% to 46% of the overall population. The Hispanic population reached 46.7 million in 2007 and will continue to rise to 132.8 million by 2050 (Bernstein & Edwards, 2008). The Hispanic population will represent 30% of the US population in2008 to 65.7 million in 2050 compared to 15% in 2008. The Black population will increase from 41.1 million in 2008 to 65.7 million in 2050 while the Asian population will increase from 15.5 million to 40.6 million. While the White, non-Hispanic population will grow from 199.8 million in 2008 to 203.3. million in 2050, the White non-Hispanic population will represent 46% less than half, of the US population in 2050 (para 8).

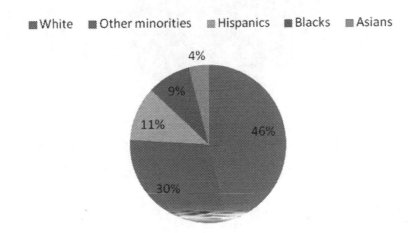

Figure 1. Population growth in the United States (1997-2008)

Betts et al. (2009) provided statistics on current minority enrollment when "comparing current demographics for administrators, faculty, and governing boards" (para. 9). The statistics showed that although minority students are 35% of the total enrollment in higher education, the administrative employment pool is disproportionately represented toward this minority enrollment (see Figure 3).

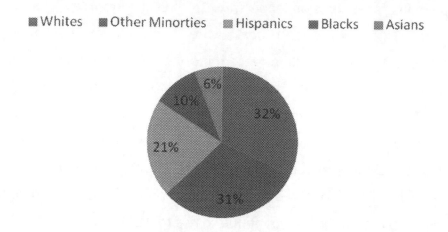

Figure 2. Population projected growth in the United States (2008-2050)

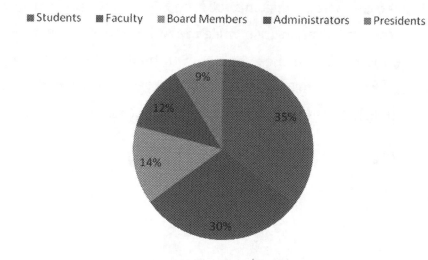

Figure 3. Minority leadership represented in colleges
related to minority student Enrollment (2009)

Betts et al. (2009) reported:

Within the US population 34% of the current population is minority and approximately 35% of the current student population enrolled in higher education is minority (Chronicle of Higher Education, 2008).

- 14% of college and university presidents (ACE, 2007);
- 19% of executive, managerial, and administrative staff (Chronicle of Higher Education, 2008),
- 22% of full-time faculty members minorities (Chronicle of Higher Education, 2008)
- 25% of part-time faculty members (Chronicle of Higher Education, 2008)
- 22% of governing board members at public colleges and universities (Association for Governing Boards, n.d.); and
- 12% of governing board members at independent colleges and universities. (Association for Governing Boards, n.d., para 9) (Figure 2)

Because of the impending leadership crisis, global and technological trends, and projected demographic shifts and changes affecting higher education, community college presidents are at an impasse, and must confront these major changes occurring within surrounding communities (Goldrick-Rab et al., 2009). Community college presidents must initiate leadership development programs to equip new leaders to mirror population growths, both racial and cultural. Betts et al. (2009) made a very important statement that related directly to this current research when they said:

> The likely wave of impending retirements among presidents presents a unique opportunity to further diversify the leadership of American higher education. This will require both that a diverse pool of talented leaders are ready and willing to ascend to the presidency and that institutions become more willing to select leaders that do not fit the traditional profile. (p. 58)

Higher education reform is in the making and presidents of higher education institutions must be prepared to commit to the "new leadership wave" (Chappell, 2008, p. 1) by including minorities in key leadership positions that will provide for best leadership initiatives. The best leadership initiatives can be developed through leadership development programs and succession plans that will lead to a more educated society and citizenry. In fact, according to President Obama, "America cannot lead in the 21ˢᵗ century unless we have the best educated, most competitive workforce in the world. And that's the kind of workforce---and the kind of citizenry—to which we must be committed" (Obama, 2009).

Role of Community College Presidents Past and Present

The governance of early established community colleges was set forth by governing boards, stipulations from grants, and faculty. The first presidents were men and they were not considered high profile leaders in the community college arena (Towsend, & Twombly, 2001).

Losco and Fife (2000) stated:

One of the true oddities of reviewing the literature on higher-education leadership is to hear a steady drumbeat about the lack of high profile academic leaders in America. The names drawn from the past have always been the same: Robert Hutchins, Clark Kerr, William Rainey Harper, Charles Elliott, and occasionally a few others. But then the list stops (Chait, 1998: 39-41). Perhaps there was a period of time when there were these great outspoken men (and they were all men). Certainly there were fewer competitors for headlines, and the job of the university or college president was far less demanding and busy. (p. 162)

According to the literature review, the leadership role of early community college presidents was less charismatic, less transformational and the leadership duties were to pass down a set of rules and regulations set forth by governing boards. Early community college presidents were austerely leading from the top down with a set of rules, processes, and regulations set forth by governing boards, namely governance. Earlier community college presidents were not known for being visionaries, charismatic, and/or transformational leaders (Altbach, Berdahl & Gumport, 1999; Baker, Dudziak, &

Tyler, 1994; Goodchild & Wechsler, 1997; Lopez-Molina, 2008). The role of the community college president has evolved as has the role of the community college over decades. Lopez Molina (2008) followed the path of the role of the presidents in the community college and stated:

> As the role of the president in the community college has developed over generations, so has their leadership styles; from managers, to collaborators, to meeting the needs of the millennium generation, globalization, and technological advancements of the institutions they lead and serve. (p. 15)

Trends such as globalization and technological advancements have indubitably influenced the role of community college presidents. Currently, community college presidents are expected to be visionaries, charismatic, trend setters, and transformational leaders (Fulton, Calkins, & Milling, 2005; Lopez-Molina, 2008). Losco and Fife (2000) identified the role of current community college presidents when they stated:

> A cursory review of recent literature would suggest strongly that today's presidents are far from silent. Whether the topic is alcohol abuse on campus, leadership in the modern era, the abuse of power, or the details of professional disciplines, presidents are writing and speaking at an undiminished rate. And they are speaking out more directly than ever on issues such as AIDS, gay-lesbian rights, domestic violence, and racism. Principled statements by presidents abound whenever a violent or a tragic event occurs. The marketplace of ideas and the media environment are more crowded than before; often these voices do not reach beyond their localized audience. (p. iii)

Community colleges continue to survive, but not without controversy from governance to governance. Alfred (1994) perceived: "Governance, closely related to concepts of administration, management, decision making and leadership, is one of the most widely discussed and misunderstood subjects in community college education today" (p.245). Alfred (1994) cited a Carnegie report that recognized governance as a "procedure that guides behavior for the common good" (p. 556). If past community college leaders were expected to lead for the common good, then current community college leaders must not only be prepared to lead for the common good, but also be expected to help prepare future leaders for the common good.

Review of the literature demonstrated that the necessity for higher education degrees has lessened in community college administration which makes for an opportunity for current leaders to adopt leadership development strategies. Alfred (1994) pointed out:

> At a time when the responsibilities of community college leaders require a skill set and knowledge base more complex than ever before, when the average age of senior administrators is rising, and when almost half of current presidents expect to retire in the next decade, the number of graduate degrees awarded in community college administration has plummeted. (p. 27)

With less qualified leaders to replace baby boomers, and the need for administrators to become educational leaders, how can community colleges change from governance to leadership and transform community colleges into higher education institutions that are lead by leaders instead of administrators following a set of rules? This is the challenge for community college presidents in this century.

Leadership Defined

Leaders of community colleges must be aware of the complexity of leadership and its many definitions in order to be prepared for the challenges that lie ahead. Since the definition of leadership was coined in the 1900s, many scholars have tried to define it. Definitions for leadership range from simple to complex. Warren G. Bennis (2000), expert and scholar on leadership, defined leadership as the role of someone who "creates a compelling vision, one that takes people to a new place, and the ability to translate that vision into reality." (p. 6) Bennis' (2000) definition of leadership portrayed the leader as the only one who is responsible for reaching the goal. It did not take into consideration the responsibility of anyone else to participate because only the leader will be able to transform vision into reality.

Conversely, John Gardner's (1990) definition of leadership concluded, "Leadership is a process of persuasion or example by which an individual (or leadership team) induces a group to pursue objectives held by the leader or shared by the leader and his or her followers" (p. 1). Gardner's (1990) definition of leadership included objectives, teams, and followers as important parts working together with a leader as valuable parts of the leadership process. Gardner's (1990) definition of leadership generates essence. After searching intensely to answer the question of what leadership is, Rosenbach and Taylor (1998) defined the meaning of leadership thusly:

> So the question remains, what is leadership and how can it be defined? I believe that leadership is a delicate combination of the process, the techniques of leadership, the person, the specific talents and traits of a/the leader, and the general requirements of the job itself. I am convinced that although the concept of leadership can and must be distinguishable and definable separately from our understanding of what and who leaders are, the phenomenon of leadership can only be known and measured in the particular instantiation of a leader doing a job. In other words, while the terms "leadership" and "leader" are not synonymous, the reality of leadership cannot be separated from the person as leader and the job of leadership. (p. 6)

Although Rosenbach and Taylor (1998) defined leadership, their definition was too broad and it is clear that they were shaping their definition to fit their "believed" version. Unlike Rosenbach and Taylor (1998), some scholars concur that the definition of leadership is indefinable. For example, Aldrich (2003) concluded:

> Getting two advocates to agree on a definition of leadership seems impossible. Covey, Blanchard, PDI, DDI, Kotter, and Achieve Global (just to name a few) competed tooth-and-nail. Many consultants have tried (and failed) to turn leadership into a cookbook-style skill, handing out recipes for anyone to follow. Meanwhile, thousands of academics have heaped layers of philosophical debate

that make leadership indefinable, almost magical. David Gergen, director of Harvard's Center for Public Leadership, worries, "Had Roosevelt and Churchill not rallied the Western democracies, and civilization might have perished." That sets the leadership bar high for the rest of us, without helping us know how they did it. (para. 4)

A precise definition for leadership may never be agreed upon, but the literature review revealed that leadership scholars will continue to discuss and grapple over its meaning. Chemers (1997) defined leadership as "a process of social influence in which one person is able to enlist the aid and support of others in the accomplishment of a common task" (p.1). He further stated that

Although this specification seems relatively simple, the reality of leadership is very complex. Intrapersonal factors (i.e., thoughts and emotions) interact with the interpersonal processes (i.e., attraction, communication, influence) to have effects on a dynamic external environment. Each of these aspects brings complexity to the leadership process. (p. 1)

The meaning of leadership has evolved from the heroic characteristics of one person to a process that involves leader and followers working toward a common goal. Gardner (1990) stated:

In any established group, individuals fill different roles, and one of the roles is that of leader. Leaders cannot be thought of apart from the historic context in which they arise, the setting in which they function (e.g., elective political office) and the system over which they preside. (e.g., a particular city or state) (p. 1)

Leadership is a process that involves many factors including everyone who is engaged in the process of reaching a common goal. Notwithstanding, the context in which a leader is chosen or needed must take precedence over his personal agenda and must be related to the common goal of the group or cause. Gardner (1990) concluded, "Effective leaders tap those (motives) that serve the purposes of collective action in pursuit of shared goals. They accomplish the alignment of individual and group goals" (p. 14).

The definition of leadership will still be debated in the future and leaders of today and tomorrow must embrace the meaning of leadership and determine, as leaders, what leadership style works best within the society, organization, or institution in which they lead. The meaning of leadership is evolving and ever growing. As long as the meaning cannot be defined adequately, then it must be understood that there is more to 'leadership" than what scholars can determine at this time. The definitions that scholars assign to leadership are parts of the totality of leadership. Scholars and leaders alike will have to observe and pause until this phenomenon called- leadership- is fully grown and there are no more pieces to affix, and then we will know the complete and true meaning of leadership. But leadership is more than a definition. It is the energy source within leaders who change, deliver, and create anew.

From Governance to Leadership in Community Colleges

The vision for the development of community colleges began with William Rainey Harper (1856-1906) who believed that students who graduated from high school would benefit academically by attending a two-year junior college and familiarize themselves with advanced learning without having to completely immerse into a higher education university where tasks of academia could be very rigorous and fastidious. Harper believed that everyone should have access to higher education. Some people believed that Harper's influence was received because it would protect universities as higher educational research institutions and the masses would be directed to the community colleges, thus leaving universities for individuals who were prepared to attend research-oriented universities. Harper's ideology and vision for the establishment of junior colleges lead to the founding of Joliet Junior College in 1901. To some, Harper's founding of the first two-year junior college in higher education may be comparable to Alexander Fleming's contribution to medicine with his discovery of penicillin in 1928. The two-year junior college transformed higher education and the results have left indelible footprints in the American higher educational system. (Firestein, 2009)

Leadership Core Competencies

Today's community college presidents are facing more challenges than their predecessors did. In order for current community college presidents to meet the demands of their constituents both internally and externally, they must equip themselves with leadership competencies that produce effective leadership. Based on findings by The American Association of Community Colleges, the six core leadership competencies for effective community college leaders include communication, collaboration, community college advocacy, professionalism, organizational strategy, and management (AACC, 2005). In 2008, the Council for the Study of Community College (CSCC) surveyed doctoral graduates to determine what percentage of graduates had developed the six leadership competency domains identified in the AACC 2005 study (organizational strategy, resource management, communication, collaboration, advocacy, and professional). The CSCC 2008 study revealed:

> While 146 respondents (96%) indicated that their programs included one or more courses in leadership, slightly fewer, 133 (88.1%) indicated that leadership skills were part of their graduate education, and only 82 (53.6%) said that developing leadership competencies was the primary reason for doing graduate work. The major of respondents indicated that their current graduate training was "moderately/extremely" helpful in developing each of the six competency domains identified by AACC: organizational strategy 82.9%, resource management 59.2, communication 85.6, collaboration 89.5, advocacy 74.6% and professional 88.8 percent (para. 8)

Although this CSCC research study provided promising results as related to presidential leaders in community colleges being prepared with the core competencies set forth by the AACC (2005) study, other studies showed that future leaders in community colleges were lacking in other core competencies that are needed in community colleges. One such study is noted by Duree (2008). Duree's study clearly showed that community college presidents and future college leaders are not well prepared to lead in other essential areas. For example, Duree (2008) stated:

...there were significant gaps in preparation on a set of issues that are likely to be essential for community college presidents in the coming years. Two of the five respondents, for instance, "did not rate themselves prepared for or well-prepared to take an entrepreneurial stance in seeking ethical alternative funding sources," at a time when two-year colleges are under increasing pressure to replace declining state and local funding. (para. 7)

He stated further, "A third of the presidents said they came into their first jobs unprepared to demonstrate "cultural competence in a global society," and a third said their pre-president training did not prepare them to be "transformational leaders," (para. 10).

Duree's (2008) goal in his research study was to "find out how well prepared community college presidents were for the biggest challenges they face in their jobs, with the hope of assessing where the leadership skills gaps are in the current training methods for would-be community college chiefs" (para. 2). Of the 400 college presidents surveyed, Duree (2008) found that "too many community college presidents are emerging from their doctoral programs—even those that specialize in producing community college leaders – without sufficient training in some key areas that they are likely to need during their presidencies" (para. 11).

According to Duree (2008), the problem with leadership programs for community college presidents is that

> If you look at a lot of the leadership programs, they are staffed by faculty who spent little time out in the field as community college leaders. My thought is that we truly need to build curriculums that get people through the Ph.D. program and maintain the intellectual integrity of the Ph.D., but have a real strong practitioner element, particularly in the areas in which community college leaders said they feel unprepared. (para. 13)

Although the AACC in 2005 identified six core competencies for future presidential leaders, Lopez-Molina (2008) identified another important area for the AACC to promote to future presidents. Lopez-Molina pointed out:

---while it (AACC, 2005) provides a framework of core competencies for leadership in community colleges, specifically geared toward the president, it does not provide information on the demographical nuances of minority individuals that can be valuable information in the succession planning or hiring process. (p. 18)

Lopez-Molina's (2008) study revealed that

The heritage of the different racial and ethnic populations is an untapped resource. Historically-marginalized social and economic classes represent a wealth of unrecognized creativity, often developing into loyal long-term employees (Baker & Kolb, 1993; Chau, 1991). Finally, the validation of the different political/cultural nuances will enhance the institutions' credibility and objectivity in the service area. This connection with community's elite could prove to be extremely important, particularly during levy renewal process. Nothing can be more important than understanding and sympathetic voters. (p. 94)

Indisputably, the research demonstrated that most scholars, and especially college presidents, have accepted the core competencies for future leaders that were adopted by the AACC in 2005. In 2006 the AACC reiterated the need for the six core competencies for community college leaders identified in 2005 and went on to say that,

Community colleges, like many other American institutions, are experiencing a leadership gap as many current leaders retire. Moreover, the leadership skills now required have widened because of greater student diversity, advances in technology, accountability demands, and globalization. Based on its continuing support of the development of community college leaders, AAC C has collaborated extensively with its many constituents to identify and endorse a set of competencies for community college leaders. (p. 3)

The development of leadership competencies and leadership skills for future leaders and community college leaders is paramount if community colleges continue to expand

and be a viable institution in American communities. Community college leaders and presidents must be equipped to lead and exercise the six core leadership competencies set forth by the AACC in 2005. In 2008, the CSCC asked 153 community college presidents which of the six core leadership domains was the most challenging. The CSCC (2008) produced these findings:

> The greatest challenges in rank order were: fundraising; enrollment; legislative advocacy; economic and workforce development; faculty relations; and diversity. Yet, among the competencies presidents were least prepared for in assuming their first presidency were: taking an entrepreneurial stance in seeking alternative funding sources; working effectively with legislators, board members, business leaders, and accrediting organizations; and valuing and promoting diversity, inclusion, equity, and academic excellence. The last area is the primary component of the AACC advocacy domain (para. 11).

The CSCC endorsed the six core competencies for future community college leaders and advocated for further research study. Duree (2008) specifically suggested a research study that identifies "which training resources provide the best background in the competency skill sets" (para. 12). He also recommended that individuals who are seeking presidencies in community colleges should develop personal development plans "that include participation in activities specifically targeting the competencies recommended by AACC" (para. 12). In-house leadership development programs were advocated by both the CSCC and Duree in 2008.

Leadership Development Programs

Community colleges are a vital part of America's culture as higher educational institutions. How presidents and other administrators lead within the community college sets the tone for sensitivity, student persistence, diversity enrollment, and culture. Governing boards and community college presidents should unite in requiring community college leadership to emulate the best positive leadership representation that can be offered to all students who enter the community college setting. Just as community colleges emulate the need for an educated society by having an open door policy education, the leadership styles and expectations should exceed the status quo leadership of governance. Community college governing boards and presidents can implement leadership development programs to foster the nature of quality leadership. The American Association of Community Colleges (2008) determined:

> As community colleges grapple with some of the most pressing issues they've ever faced—teacher shortages, swelling enrollments, and budget cuts, to name a few—those at the helm of the institutions are critical in determining the schools' success. Meanwhile, with scores of baby boomers on the verge of retiring, community college leadership also will be facing a shortage. Such challenges, educators say, only underscore the need for more and better community college leaders and programs to train them (p. 4)

> Leadership competencies and attributes considered necessary for future leaders in colleges and universities including community colleges are noted by researchers and scholars such as Amey & VanDerLinden, 2002; Bass, 1998; and Boggs, 2003. In 2007, Hull and Keim sent out a survey to current community college presidents to determine the nature and status of community college leadership development/succession planning programs.

They found that

> With 286 out of 389 responding for a return rate of 74% of national and regional programs, the *Chair Academy*, the *Executive Leadership initiative*, and the *Future Leaders Institute* had the highest percentages of participation by top-level community college administrators. Nearly 70% of presidents believe there is a need to expand in-house development program. (p. 689)

Hull and Keim's (2007) research study supported the fact that leadership development programs are valuable and effective to the institution's participants, departments, and the institution itself. Their research data showed that "A total of 89% of presidents thought that leadership programs were valuable to participants, 85% felt that programs were of value to participants' departments and 87% thought they were of value to the institution (p. 695).

Leadership development programs that target minorities as future leaders are the Lakin Institute for Mentored Leadership (National Council on Black American Affairs) and the Hispanic Leadership Fellows Program (National Community College Hispanic Council) (Hull & Keim, 2007, p. 699).

Lopez-Molina (2008) identified four programs that targeted minorities as future leaders.

She stated:

> The following are four of the programs designed to support minority future leaders: The National Community College Hispanic Council: A leadership development program preparing and supporting Hispanic leaders in America's community colleges (NCCHC, 2007). The Future Leaders Institute: A leadership seminar designed for mid-level administrators (AACC, 2007b; Boggs, 2004a, 2004b. The Presidents Academy: A series of convening's dedicated for professional renewal and recognition of the CEO's (AACC, 2007b), and the Executive Leadership Institute sponsored by the League for Innovation in the Community College in cooperation with The University of Texas at Austin and the American Association of Community Colleges: A series of convening's designed for future leaders and leaders in transition. (League, 2007) (p. 20)

Based on the literature review, leadership development plans provide opportunities for individuals to improve their leadership skills and/or learn new leadership skills for transforming organizations and institutions. In-house leadership development plans are those development plans that are geared toward employees who are already employed by the institutions and are geared toward learning core competencies of leadership and who are inspired to becoming effective leaders (AACC, 2006; ICCD (Institute for Community College Development), 2006; Gonzalez, Sullivan, & Phillipe,

2005). Unquestionably, the literature review identified excellent leadership development programs on the national level, but in the localized area where community colleges exists, there is not much evidence that leadership development programs are on the rise.

Currently, community college leaders are aware of leadership development programs, but few presidents are adopting them within their institutions (Hull & Keim, 2007). The AACC summit of 2004 published responses from community college leaders on leadership development plans. The purpose of the summit was to (a) define leadership development, (b) determine how it could be measured, and delivered and (c) determine what leadership development encompass. Based on the responses from the summit there were various definitions for leadership development. Dorsey (2004) concluded:

> Leadership Development is the ability to provide opportunities to grow leaders within the organization; ability to provide mentorship for up and coming leaders, ability to identify talented potential leaders, who may not know that this is their fate, ability to offer formal professional development on all topics pertinent to effectively leading an organization (leadership styles, planning and budgeting, hiring the best and the brightest, consensus building, and other topics. (p. 1)

The literature review revealed the "humanistic mentoring" approach and "servant mentoring" as possible mentoring processes are open for future discussion (Varney, 2009). The humanistic mentoring approach and servant mentoring are two possible approaches to use especially, when mentoring minorities, according to Varney and Steinbeck (2009).

Why Succession Planning in Community Colleges?

With additional budget cuts a certainty for community colleges, how can more and better prepared individuals join the community college leadership team? In order for community colleges to address succession planning for future leadership, governing boards and community college presidents must recognize two demographic issues that are the driving force behind the need for succession planning in higher education. Parkman and Beard (2008) stated:

> Democratic issues relate to the sheer number of individuals in the baby boomer cohort the retirement of the baby boomers. It is estimated that currently there are well over 60 million workers between the ages of 41 and 59 who are approaching retirement (Harrison & Hargrove 2006). Institutions will be challenged by the speed at which the current pool of experienced leaders will leave the workplace. In 2006, the first baby boomers turned 60 at a rate of 330 every hour. The rate of retirement will continue to increase as the boomers move through the next decade (U.S. Census Bureau 2008). The impact will be more significantly realized in higher education, where institutions face a decline in interest in the professorate as a whole as budget deficits are accelerating the retirement of a number of faculty members through early retirement benefits. (p. 1)

The review of the literature revealed that the baby boomer phenomenon is real and must be taken seriously, not only by industries and business sectors, but higher educational institutions must also prepare for this leadership crisis due to impending retirements. Before succession planning can be implemented successfully in community colleges, community college leaders must understand the role of the community college. Wallin, Cameron, and Sharples (2005) stated:

> Community colleges take pride in the fact that they are learning organizations. Their highest priority is teaching and learning and their most important concern is student success. Yet these same learning-centered organizations often neglect the learning needs of their internal constituencies. 'The asset that truly appreciates within any organization is people. Systems become dated. Buildings deteriorate. Machinery wears out. But people can grow, develop, and become more effective if they have a leader who understands their potential value. In the next decade, administrators and faculty hired in the high-growth 60s and 70s will be leaving the institutions they helped build. The wave of retirements of

senior level administrative and faculty leaders 'makes urgent the need to include succession planning in professional development programs. (p 2)

Wallin, Cameron, and Sharples (2005) defined succession planning as

...a process by which an organization assures necessary and appropriate leadership for the future through a talent pipeline with the capabilities of sustaining an institution's long-term goals. In other words, it is having the right people in the right place at the right time. (p. 2)

If a community college expects to have the right people, at the right place, at the right time, a strategic internal leadership assessment must be conducted before choosing or implementing leadership development strategies for succession planning. Ruse and Jansen (2008) suggested that the organization

first determine the type of talent needed to implement institutional strategy by translating that strategy into operational requirements and identifying and prioritizing the talent segments and roles that will be key to achieving these requirement; secondly, figure the net number of people needed over the term of the institution's strategic/operational plan; thirdly, identify the talent gaps and priorities and determine the best approach for closing the gaps by looking at the relative size, strategic value and urgency of each gap and examining the costs (direct and indirect) of hiring versus developing talent; and finally, decide what actions/investments the institutions should take to align its overall strategy, Human Resource strategy and talent management processes with operational requirements. This involves focusing on the talent management processes that are most critical to addressing the need in each talent segment, assessing the performance of each and recommending actions to improve performance. (p. 2)

Ruse and Jansen (2008) addressed succession planning as "using human capital planning to predict future talent needs" (p. 1). Although Ruse and Jansen (2008) identified specific action steps for colleges and universities to implement, they did not address what secession planning is not. However, Wallin, Cameron, and Sharples (2005) did. They declared:

> It is important to define what succession planning is not. It is not an entitlement; it is not a job guarantee; it is not an extension of the 'good ole' boy network. On the contrary, succession planning, when coupled with intentional and targeted leadership development, seeks out diverse candidates and casts a wider net within the organization. Succession planning provides opportunities, while clearly recognizing that not every participant in succession planning activities will move into a leadership role. Finally, succession planning does not preclude bringing in talent from outside the organization. (p. 2)

Wallen, Cameron, and Sharples (2005) clearly identified that diversity should be a part of succession planning coupled with opportunity for candidates to compete for leadership positions.

Even though employees who participate in leadership development programs may not obtain a leadership position they are benefiting from leadership development training, which will enhance their leadership understanding and capabilities and boost their courage to seek higher educational leadership positions at other institutions.

During the next decade community college leaders will be faced with many challenges in replacing the many potential retirees. Succession planning is a must for those community colleges that would like to remain successful in the future. Succession planning offers many benefits, but conversely, may have some problems as well. What benefits can community college presidents expect to gain if they decide to launch succession planning at their college? One of the benefits of succession planning is to identify potential leaders. Moreover, it will train and develop those leaders who are already at the institution and who will be qualified to lead, instead of selecting replacement leaders from outside the institution who may or may not know the internal vision or mission of the college. Also, staff members who are involved in succession planning will feel appreciated for their experience while working and growing within the community college. Available leadership positions can be discerned, created and targeted well in advance.

One of the best benefits of succession planning is to be able to identify leadership gaps within the leadership framework. Leadership gaps occur when potential employees are not qualified or trained to replace leaders who are leaving the institution or retiring. Succession planning provides an avenue to identify leadership gaps ahead of time and the institution can prepare for future leaders and thrive. Others may think they are left out if they are not selected to participate in the succession planning process. Finally, minorities may think that they should not participate if they do not see minorities being selected after they complete the succession planning process. All programs offer negative and positive rewards. However, the literature review demonstrated that if community colleges are going to remain effective and progressive in the future, they must consider succession planning (AACC, 2004, 2006; Betts et al. 2009; Clunies, 2007; Leubsdorf, 2006; Lopez-Molina, 2008; Viniar 2008; Wallen, Cameron, & Sharples, 2005).

Leadership Types for Transforming Community Colleges

There are many leadership styles such as charismatic, autocratic, visionary, heroic, democratic, situational, transformational, and servant leader, to name a few. Models of leadership include paradigms of leadership and how leaders make decisions in organizations and institutions. For the purpose of this current research servant leadership and transformational leadership will be discussed. In addition, Bolman and Deal's (2003) four leadership frames will be discussed in order to demonstrate how these four frames support different leadership styles needed for transforming community colleges.

Servant Leadership

A "servant leader" is a leader who collaborates with his followers and includes their interests, visions, hopes and goals. Lopez-Molina (2008) traced the foundation for servant leadership. She stated:

The concept and practice of servant leader or servant hood is found as early as in biblical times: The leader, pastor, and "chief shepherd of the flock" (1 Peter 5: 4). While the model and practice of servant leadership has been central to the Christian faith over the centuries "called to serve, rather than be served" (Mathew 20:28, the practice of serving others is also central to the concept of the transformational leader (Sendjaya & Sarros, 2002; Block, 1993; Ford, 1991) (p. 23).

She went on to point out that servant leadership was defined by Robert Greenleaf in 1970.

Lopez-Molina (2008) stated:

The concept of servant leadership has more recently been defined by Greenleaf (1970; 2003). "Servant Leader," or the objective of servant leadership, is to stimulate thought and action for building a better, more caring society. In searching for a servant leader with experience and scholarship in a president for a community college, the servant leader is also one who promotes social justice and is unconditional in doing so (Greenleaf, 1970, 2003; Kim, 2002; Spears 2002, 2003). (p. 23)

According to the literature review, the servant leader model of leadership is gaining support, especially as a leadership model for inclusion and diversity. Page (2003) reiterated:

The most powerful theory of leadership that is supportive of a diverse culture is servant leadership, a theory that first came into prominence when Greenleaf (1970) published *Servant as Leader*. In fact, the Greenleaf Center for Servant Leadership has produced numerous conferences and articles on the subject. Spears (1998) discusses Greenleaf and define servant leadership as the creation of a community that 'puts serving others-including employees, customers, and community-as the number one priority.' (p. 79)

Page (2003) compiled five principles to promote diversity in academic leadership. They are:

> (a) commitment to understanding other cultures and the value of diversity in leadership positions, (b) understanding and commitment to basic values that flow through the organization, (c) creation of a culture of trust where the diversity organization has a high level of respect for all cultures presented, (d) conscious development of strategies to recruit or provide mobility for women and ethnic minorities within the organization, and (e) a willingness to be accountable for the success or failure of promoting diversity within the academic leadership-accountable for monitoring and mentoring the leader. (p. 81)

The five principles conveyed the importance of community college leaders including diversity in the mission of the college and reflect the minority population in the leadership pool. Page (2003) reemphasized the following:

> The first building block on which an institution can promote diversity within the academic leadership is to employ leaders who recognize that they must serve all constituents to secure followers from any constituency. Leaders must understand the culture and value diversity and as Covey says 'have respect for the differences in people.' (p. 80)

Lopez-Molina (2008) also promoted and demonstrated the value of college presidents becoming servant leaders. She stated:

> In efforts to be a servant leader in its truest sense in an institution of higher education, it is critical that a president of a community college develops a sound understanding of the needs of the constituency they serve and lead (Greenleaf, 1970, 2003). The practice of servant leadership, one of moral persuasion, will enable the president in higher education to transform their practices internally and externally to the institution and communities creating servant leaders, renewing the respect for human life and human spirit. (Greenleaf, 1970, 2003) (p. 24)

Transformational Leadership

The literature review revealed that a servant leader can also be congruent with transformational leaders (Polleys, 2002; Lopez-Molina, 2008). Lopez-Molina (2008) viewed the transformational leader as one who "successfully facilitates the change in composition, structure, character or condition of an organization such as the culture and climate" (p. 21). When transformational leadership and servant leadership are combined to create a moral environment where the expectations are raised for both the leaders and the followers, Lopez Molina (2008) identifies it as "extraordinary transformational leadership" (p. 22). Avolio and Bass, (2002) agreed. They concluded:

> True transformational leaders raise the level of moral maturity of those whom they lead. They convert their followers into leaders. They broaden and enlarge the interests of those whom they lead. They motivate their associates, colleagues, followers, clients, and even their bosses to go beyond their individual self-interests for the good of the group, organization, or society. (p. 1)

Most leadership types can be used for organizational change, but which leadership models can produce the most results when leaders are trying to achieve organizational change? The literature review showed that leaders who are transformational leaders are viewed as highly effective leaders (Avolio & Bass, 2005, p. 198).

Bolman and Deal's Frames

Bolman and Deal (2003) described four leadership types or frames and detail how leaders can utilize them when making important decisions within organizations and institutions. These frames are: (a) structural, (b) human resource, (c) political, and (d) symbolic.

Structural frame. According to Bolman and Deal (2003), the structural frame of leadership requires that community college presidents build a structural foundation by establishing the following:

Clarifying goals, attending to the relations between structure and environment, and developing a clearly defined structure appropriate to what needs to be done. Without a workable structure, people become unsure about what they are supposed to be doing. The result is confusion, frustration, and conflict. In an effective organization, individuals are relatively clear about their responsibilities and their contribution. Policies, linkages, and lines of authority are straightforward and widely accepted. With the right structure-one that people understand and accept-the organization can achieve its goals, and individuals can see their role in the big picture. (p. 322)

Through this structural frame, community college presidents can implement a structural plan that will clarify the mission and goals of the community college with specific emphasis to exceed the expectations of state and federal agencies. Furthermore, community college presidents can establish and define the roles of each higher level position and incorporate a strategy that will include minorities as a valuable component to leadership positions. If presidents employ organizational structure and change, they will clearly see what role is expected of them and minorities will have an opportunity to develop interest in becoming part of the higher educational leadership arena. By working through the structural lens of leadership, community college presidents can ultimately acquire local leadership autonomy. Bolman and Deal (2003) concluded: "Understanding the complexity and variety of design possibilities can help create structures that work for, rather than against, both the people and the purposes of organizations" (p. 76).

Human resource frame. The human resource frame is about how people are treated in the community college at all levels including students, faculty, support staff, department heads, deans, executives, vice presidents and presidents. According to Bolman and Deal (2003) the human resource frame is based on four assumptions. They are:

(a) organizations exist to serve human needs rather than the reverse: (b) people and organizations need each other. Organizations need ideas, energy, and talent; and people need careers, salaries, and opportunities; (c) when the fit between individual and system is poor, one or both suffer. Individuals are exploited or exploit the organization-or both become victims; and (b) a good fit benefits both. Individuals find meaningful and satisfying work, and organizations get the talent and energy they need to succeed. (p. 115)

Community college presidents' actions and decisions have direct impact on the community college and the people in and outside the community college. It would be a benefit to community college presidents if they embraced creative and powerful ways to align individual and organizational needs. By doing so, they will embark on a course that reflects the human resource frame's core assumptions by viewing, as Bolman and Deal stated, the workforce as an investment rather than a cost (p. 129).

By leading through the human resource frame, community college presidents can contribute to major improvements in the community colleges employee morale, students' achievements, culture, and growth of the community college because job satisfaction improves productivity, according to Bolman and Deal (2003).

Political frame. When North Carolina's Beverly Perdue ran for governor in 2008, she promised voters that she would provide equal access to community colleges for all North Carolina high school graduates. After she took the oath of office, she publicly announced that due to the economic crisis, she could not fulfill her promise. This is but one example that community colleges are at the mercy of political power, conflict, and community coalitions. Knowing this, community college presidents must understand and be aware of five political assumptions described by Bolman and Deal (2003). They are:

> (a) organizations are coalitions of diverse individuals interest groups; (b) there are enduring difference among coalition members in values, beliefs, information, interests, and perceptions of reality; (c) most important decisions involve allocating scarce resources-who gets what; (d) scarce resources and enduring differences make conflict central to organizational dynamics and underline power as the most important asset; and (e) goals and decisions emerge from bargaining, negotiation, and jockeying for position among competing stakeholders. (p. 186)

When using the political paradigm, presidents of community colleges must lead carefully, yet boldly, and not compromise integrity or inflict human suffering on employees. Conflict must be dealt with cautiously so as to improve the overall operations of the community colleges. Bolman and Deal (2003) stated:

> Even more important than the amount of conflict is how it is managed. Poor conflict management leads to the kind of infighting and destructive power struggle...But well-handled conflict can stimulate the creativity and innovation that make an organization a livelier, more adaptive, and more effective place. (p. 198)

In times of political conflict, community college presidents can be influential by using their power constructively and not abusively. Bolman and Deal (2003) concluded: "Constructive politics is a possibility-----indeed, a necessary possibility if we are to create institutions and societies that are both just and efficient" (p. 201).

Symbolic frame. When community college presidents create institutions that are just and efficient, they become symbols in the community. The symbolic frame of leadership incorporates the view of employees, community at large, and everyone's view of what they see in the community college environment. Bolman and Deal (2003) stated that the symbolic frame focuses on how humans make sense of the world in which they live and work. The five assumptions of the symbolic frame are:

> (a) what is the most important is not what happens but what it means; (b) activity and meaning are loosely coupled; events have multiple meanings because people interpret experience differently; (c) in face of widespread uncertainty and ambiguity, people create symbols to resolve confusion, increase predictability, find direction, and anchor hope and faith; (d) many events and processes are more important for what is expressed than what is produced. They form a cultural tapestry of secular myths, heroes, and heroines, rituals, ceremonies, and stories that help people find purpose and passion in their personal work lives; and (e) culture is the glue that holds an organization together and unites people around shared values and beliefs. (p. 242)

When the community college presidents make decisions from the symbolic paradigm, they are making decisions based on the culture of the community college; its beliefs, symbols, and values. In this century, community college presidents have the opportunity to improve the value of the community college and to live out the mission and vision upon which it was created to represent all peoples in the community by continuing to provide an open door policy education and offer leadership opportunities to minorities for future leadership roles and representation in the higher educational workplace. Through symbolic leadership, the community college can become a place of unity, cohesiveness, and clarity where people accept the past, become change agents in the present, and passes down innovation and creativity to the next generation.

Whichever type of leadership community college presidents use as their leadership paradigm, it is critical that these community college presidents determine how to replace the potential baby boomers who will be retiring within the next decade. This is the time for community college presidents to embrace change and implement leadership development programs that will benefit the employees of the community college as well as mirror the growth of communities by including minority leadership. Bolman and Deal's (2003) paradigms of leadership can be utilized within the community college setting as well as other organizations. Through the structural, human resource, symbolic, and/or political leadership frames, community college presidents can practice autonomy and implement tactics and strategies for leadership development, open door policies for students, community involvement, and exceed the expectations of local agencies, both state and federal.

Lopez Molina (2008) concluded: "If the institution is authentically interested in addressing the leadership gap challenge and disparity of minorities within their institution, it must be willing to motivate, engage, and inspire others to facilitate the transformation process involved" (p. 26). Community college leaders not only have the opportunity to begin leadership development programs, but begin leadership programs that are developed with a mentoring component that embraces minority leadership to ward against the impending leadership crisis.

Mentoring in Community Colleges for Change

Review of the literature presented not only an impending leadership crisis in higher education leadership (AACC, 2005; Eddy, 2009; Shultz, 2006), but also a leadership mentoring shortage for underrepresented populations in community colleges (; Eddy, 2009; Esters & Mosby, 2007). The underrepresented groups include minorities such as African Americans, American Indians, Asians, and Hispanics. Succession planning and leadership development programs are indispensable when it comes to transforming community colleges and significantly to thwart the impending leadership crisis, however; mentoring can also be advantageous within succession planning and leadership development programming. As community college presidents embrace succession planning and leadership development programs, they must also be mindful of the underrepresented populations in higher leadership roles in community colleges. Lopez-Molina (2008) pointed out:

As the profiles of institutions of higher education have changed over time, so has the need for indentifying racially and culturally underrepresented leaders as to be more reflective of the constituencies served. Understanding and managing cultures in the ever changing nature of how institutions of higher education conduct business is key in today's global marketplace. (p. 43)

To embrace these challenges, community college leaders need only to revisit mentoring as part of the leadership development programs for transforming change and culture in community colleges, especially in the rural areas. This section will discuss concepts of mentoring, types of mentoring, and how mentoring can be used as a transformational tool to embrace diversity and underrepresented groups within succession and leadership development programs in community colleges in both rural and urban areas.

Gener (2006) stated:

Lately the idiom of mentoring has been making the rounds. As a training tool and educational philosophy, it has gained fresh currency and unusual traction in professional theatres, university settings and conservatory programs across the country. Formal mentoring programs with elaborate machineries of selection, screening, interviewing, designation, administration and funding have cropped up--and their proliferation in the recent decades militates against an orthodox view of mentoring, which insists that, in the performing arts, there can be no single ideology or paradigm of what constitutes the practice. Because mentoring is not a new custom--it dates back at least to its ancient Greek etymology in Book 2 of Homer's Odyssey--many existing programs are being reconfigured to address its renewed appeal. (p. 1)

Darwin and Palmer (2009) defined mentoring as the "process of influencing and fostering the intellectual development of students and career aspirations of staff" (p. 125).

Lopez-Molina (2008) suggested that mentoring becomes a transformational process. Within this process, community college leaders have an obligation to reflect leadership that corresponds to the study population. Lopez-Molina stated, "Developing and institutionalizing comprehensive and integrative leadership development programs that include coaching, mentoring, and succession planning will give community colleges the opportunity to preserve and further the legacy of their rich history" (p. 41). She went on to say, "Mentoring, coaching, and leadership development programs for employees as future leaders of institutions must consider the individual's cultural background as well as their experiences, as significant in the planning, developing, and customizing of professional development programs" (p. 41).

The review of the literature clearly provided an unequivocal distinction of the underrepresented populations in higher education leadership positions and especially a lack of mentoring programs in which to develop pathways to encourage minority leadership (Rendon, 2003). The underrepresented groups in leadership roles also include African Americans, Asians, Latinos, and women, in both urban and rural areas (Eddy, 2009; Esters & Mosby, 2007).

In 2006, The Chronicle of Higher Education published "A Profile of Community-College Presidents." It was found that of the 61 % responses received from 545 presidents, 54% stated that they mentor someone who would like to become president. Based on their demographics and profiles of college presidents reporting, the information showed that when it comes to race representation, 81.2% are White, 8.1% are African American, 5.8% are Hispanic, 2.4% are Native American, and 1.5%t are Asian. The data revealed that 72% of the presidents are male and 28% are female.

The demographics that depicted student population in the literature review are not in keeping with the leadership representation presented by Rendon, 2003. Specifically, since 1987, minority enrollment numbers have continued to increased in community colleges with an expected enrollment increase of about 47% of the student body by the year 2025 (Andrews & Fonseci, 1998; Szelenyi, 2001). Based on the enrollment statistics, then, why are minority populations underrepresented in both faculty positions as well as in leadership roles?

Rendon (2003) explained one reason why minority populations may be underrepresented. She stated:

Colleges and universities have not understood the population with which they are dealing. In the past, the United States has tended to view issues of race and ethnicity as a black-white divide, effectively dismissing or marginalizing the issues of other groups. As a result, most institutions of higher education have not considered that the members of many racial and ethnic groups have complex identities based on class, generational status, gender, sexual orientation, ethnic identification, abilities, spirituality, etc. Some Latinos are biracial or multiracial and resist being labeled as belonging to one single ethnic or racial group. (p. 2)

The literature review revealed startling information which showed that mentoring at community colleges is often used only for promoting "at risk students" and improving college attendance. Valeau, and Boggs (2004) had this to say about mentoring programs in community colleges:

There are relatively few structured mentor programs within the community college sector designed specifically for aspiring junior-level administrators. Although a number of article have called for the development of such programs (Jones, 1998) a review of the ERIC database reveals fewer than 25 articles, studies, and other publications that describe such programs. In large part, this sparse literature reflects that the majority of mentor programs in education focus almost exclusively on promoting college attendance and completion among at-risk youth (e. g., Pagan & Edwards-Wilson, 2003; Peterman, 2003) (p. 2).

Through mentoring, community college leaders can change the culture and climate of their institutions. Mentoring for leadership success is contentious. To be successful, community college leaders must be vigorous in searching for mentoring models that show success. One mentor model that the literature revealed is the American Association of California Community College Administrators (AACCA) established in 1988. This mentoring program was established to promote career development of mentees from underrepresented groups. According to Valeau and Boggs (2004):

A prerequisite to fostering a full understanding of mentor programs is developing a definition that applies equally to the community college setting and business or pre-college programs. Because the AACCA program is one of the oldest planned mentor programs for community colleges professionals in the nation, operating in a state with nearly 10% of the nations' community colleges, data drawn from a careful analysis of the program offer a basis for developing a broader definition of the mentoring process. (p. 4)

Valeau and Boggs (2004) detailed how a mentor is selected within the AACCA mentoring plan:

An administrator who may desire to serve as mentor must begin by completing ACCCA's mentor application form. This form requires that the applicant commit to assist a protégé in developing mastery of those skills and competencies unique to a senior-level administrative position within a community college. Additionally each application must not only provide a detailed description of the specific values, competencies, and contracts he or she will share with a protégé, but must also stipulate the amount of time he or she will commit to the program. Based on the number of accepted protégés and the best possible match between a protégé's objectives and a mentor's competencies, ACCCA matches each of the 15 to twenty protégés with a mentor for a minimum of one year. (p. 54)

Valeau and Boggs (2004) assessed the benefits of mentoring. They found that "mentoring along with broadened access to terminal degrees, not only provide for the intergenerational transfer of essential skills, knowledge, and behaviors, but also contributes to the gender and racial diversification of qualified applicants for senior-level administrative positions" (p. 2) in community colleges.

Mentoring may be an important means to success by providing formal or informal mentoring for faculty, staff, or students, especially in the case of minorities. In case of minority students, it is important for them to have mentors. As Dickey (1996b) stated:

> Mentoring cannot be overlooked when examining the various contributors to student persistence. For minority students, mentoring programs can means a difference between isolation and integration; failure and success. Social and academic integration levels of students in the higher education institution can be affected by mentoring. (p. 6)

Dickey (1996a) further pointed out that:

> Mentoring programs should be designed to ensure as much interaction as possible with departments or programs that most affect the academic and social lives of culturally diverse students. Advertising and recruitment should emphasize the reciprocal benefits of participation to enhance the image of the mentoring relationship as a partnership rather than a "missionary" one. (p. 54)

The Call for Leadership Diversity in Community Colleges

The literature review pointed the way for community colleges to address the diversity issue in community college leadership due to the growing enrollment of persons of color.

Altbach, Berdahl, and Gumport stated:

> In the decades from 1960 through the early 1990s, American colleges and universities were subject to political and judicial pressure to increase racial diversity on campus. The demographics of the American population as well as demands for access to higher education have contributed to the growth in numbers of underrepresented students. (p. 450)

Altbach, Berdahl, and Gumport (1997) featured the *Talented Ten* written by W. E. B. Dubois in 1903 in their book entitled: *History of Higher Education.* Altbach et al (1997) noted that in 1903 W. E. B. Dubois discussed the importance of diversity leadership in the American education system. Dubois questioned:

> How then can the leaders of a struggling people be trained and the hands of the risen few strengthened? There can be but one answer: The best and most capable of their youth must be schooled in the colleges and universities of the land. (p. 553)

Altbach, Berdahl, and Gumport (1997) also noted the call for diversity inclusion from Alexander Meiklejohn, the first president of Amherst College in Massachusetts from 1912 -1924, who said:

> We may not keep ourselves apart either from persons or from cultures not our own. We dare not shut our gate to our fellow-citizens or to their influence...And if they do not come, we must go out and bring them in. (p. 523)

The call for diversity inclusion in leadership positions is still echoing today in the 21st Century. According to Evelyn (2001), "many people are urging boards to select leaders with different styles and even professional backgrounds than the retiring presidents, who many complain have a state of mind mired in the 1960's and 70's" (p. 4). Evelyn (2001) also pointed out:

As minority-student population rise—they grew from 25 percent to 30 percent of community –college enrollments between 1922 and 1997-many higher education experts say that leaders must know how to deal with diversity. And if the colleges are to train workers for technology jobs, some observers advocate finding young leaders who understand and embrace the field. (p. 5)

The American Association of Community Colleges (AACC) 2008 report stated,

Community colleges are the most diverse and inclusive institutions of higher education in the United States. Community colleges serve larger percentages of African-Americans, Asian/Pacific Islanders, Hispanic Americans, Native Americans, and students with disabilities than any other segment of higher education, and well over half of community college students are women. Most of the women and minority higher education presidents are found in the ranks of American community colleges. However, progress has been slow in identifying and employing presidents who are representative of the student bodies and the communities served by the colleges. Presidents and trustees should mirror the populations on our campuses and be committed to the participation and success of all groups. (para. 4)

To increase minority leadership representation in this current economic crisis, structural changes in community college governing boards could be addressed. For example, community colleges could be grouped regionally and the state could have one board of directors for each region instead of a board of directors for each community college. A regional board of directors could offer diverse leadership opportunities that would emulate the population of the communities they serve, thus increasing diversified leadership. The trend of minority enrollment in community college is not going to decrease. The AACC (2008) report explained why:

The combination of the open door admissions policy, low tuition, and easy geographic access makes the community colleges particularly attractive to many minority students who might otherwise not contemplate college. The most dramatic pattern on the map is the southern rim of states in which minority enrollment amounts to 23 percent or more of total enrollment. The southern rim includes the states of the Deep South, with large proportions of African Americans, and the Southwestern states, where the proportion of Hispanics is high. The presence of another minority, Native Americans, is apparent inside the southern rim, especially in Arizona, New Mexico and Oklahoma, and also in the north in the Dakotas and Montana. Also in the high category are some states where the proportion of minority population in metropolitan areas is quite large -- New York, New Jersey, Illinois, and Maryland. California is both heavily metropolitan and heavily minority. (para 6)

Chapter Summary

The American Association of Community Colleges (AACC, 2002) and others (Shults, 2001; O'Banion, 2006) are aware of the impending leadership crisis facing higher education institutions. Community colleges may not be prepared to face this leadership replacement crisis. To prepare for this looming leadership crisis, it may be necessary for presidents and governing boards to develop succession plans and leadership development programs for succession leadership. These succession plans must be inclusive of interested participants and must not adhere to status quo leadership. Regardless of gender and/or race, color, religion, or sexual orientation, individuals who are employed by community colleges must be given the opportunity to participate and compete for mid- and high-level administrative positions.

Review of the literature revealed that some community colleges and other high educational institutions are not preparing for the impending leadership crisis. Lopez-Molina (2008) stated:

The analysis of the collected data indicates that senior and mid-level administrators at A, B, and C are not aware to what extent their respective institution is preparing future leaders. Although some respondents could identify a few occurrences of informal examples of mentoring, the lack of purpose-driven, long-term structured programs with adequate funding remains an anomaly. (p. 93)

Lopez-Molina's (2008) analysis clearly demonstrated that

> There is no question that the retention of key staff supervised by senior and mid-level administrators is of paramount concern; but again, without formal policy-driven protocols to guide retention efforts, the respondents could not relate succession planning to leadership development. (p. 93)

Community college presidents and governing boards must set clear guidelines for professional development and establish protocols to identify leadership gaps through succession planning. This is a viable motivational tool for potential future leaders. Because community colleges are ever growing organizations filled with diverse students from various sociological and economic backgrounds, community college presidents must represent the entire student body. More often than not, community colleges align their resources toward curriculum programs and due to scare resources and lack of funds, overlook programs that promote basic skills, vocational and occupational education; diploma and certificate program, and place more emphasis on funding curriculum programs that produce two-year associate degrees.

Goldrick-Rab et al. (2009) stated:

> A performance measurement system would help policy makers, institutions, and students stay focused, and ensure that we make the most efficient and effective use of scare resources. Research suggests that as their enrollments increase, colleges dilute the amount of resources spent on students and instruction, which in turn contributes to low completion rates. These institutions are often losers in the battle for scarce state resources, a situation that state budget crises are likely to exacerbate in coming years. (p. 5)

The future of the community college phenomenon rests in the hands of its governing boards and community college presidents, who cannot become complacent and overlook the impending leadership crisis and other major trends facing community colleges today. Wallin, Cameron, and Sharples (2005) determined:

> Colleges who genuinely commit to succession planning have the opportunity to create a dynamic roadmap to institutional sustainability while providing meaningful and targeted leadership development to motivated individuals. Boards, presidents, and senior leadership teams become more cognizant of the importance of developing leaders from within. Succession planning becomes a part of strategic planning, and leadership development is no longer peripheral to the institution but becomes integral to institutional effectiveness. Thoughtfully implemented at all levels, succession planning supports the teaching and learning mission of the college and provides effective leadership for a challenging future. Succession planning and targeted leadership development can help make America's community colleges work. (p. 4)

Chapter 1 introduced the North Carolina Community College system with its 58 community colleges serving communities in 100 counties. This review of the literature provided an overview of the complexity of leadership and how leadership scholars grapple over its meaning as it applies to organizational leaders and leaders in higher educational institutions. This literature review lead to the expansion of Lopez-Molina's (2008) research study and the comparative analysis revealed how succession planning for leadership positions is evolving in higher education. This research study added to the sparse body of literature and examined how eight community colleges identified and prepared future leaders in North Carolina.

CHAPTER 3. METHODOLOGY

Introduction

The purpose of this research study was to replicate the Lopez-Molina (2008) study which determined how select community colleges contributed to the development of future community college leaders. This current research study expanded the research from three community colleges in three different states to eight selected community colleges within the North Carolina Community College System, and determined how the selected community colleges contributed to leadership development programs. Furthermore, this current research investigated if the demographics of employees serving in the selected North Carolina community colleges were reflected in leadership positions as well. Finally, this research determined if the selected North Carolina community colleges are cognizant of the impending leadership crisis as forecasted by The American Association of Community College (2006) and others.

This current research study used mixed methods research methodology. Creswell and Plano Clark (2008) identified five important elements that researchers should consider when using the mixed methods paradigm. They are: (a) "defining the problem and searching the literature; (b) identifying the research design; (c) identifying data sources and selecting the participants; and (d) identifying or constructing data collection instruments and methods; and (e) analyzing, interpreting, and reporting results" (p.77).

Mixed methods research studies, according to Creswell and Plano Clark (2007), are "studies that are products of the pragmatist paradigm and that combine the qualitative and quantitative approaches within different phases of the research process" (p. 22). They went on to say that

Mixed method research is a research design with philosophical assumptions as well as methods of inquiry. As a methodology, it involves philosophical assumptions that guide the direction of the collection and analysis of data and the mixture of qualitative and quantitative data in a single study or series of studies. Its central premise is that the use of quantitative and qualitative approaches in combination provides a better understanding of research problems than either approach alone. (p. 5)

In this current mixed methods research study a survey was used to collect the quantitative data and data collected from interviews was the qualitative part of the study. This researcher chose mixed methods research because it combined survey (numerical) and interview (descriptive) methodology to get the best results from the research study. This research study was a replication study of Lopez-Molina's (2008) research study. The survey instrument was divided into two parts. Part I requested personal data from senior administrative participants. The survey instrument (see Appendix A) and follow-up interviews (Appendix B), as used in Lopez-Molina's (2008) study, was the guiding instruments for this current research study.

Why Educational Research?

According to Gall, Gall, and Borg (2003) educational research is paramount because "educational research develops new knowledge about teaching, learning, and educational administration. This new knowledge is of value because it will lead eventually to the improvement of educational practice" (p. 3). Mixed methods research has gained momentum in the research arena and his advocated by Creswell and Plano Clark (2007). They stated:

From our collective research experiences and conversations with colleagues, we have found that a mixed methods approach has interdisciplinary appeal to many researchers. These researchers hold increasingly diverse worldviews and tackle complex issues and problems that beg for a blending of qualitative and quantitative data. Hence, mixed method designs provide researchers, across research disciplines, with rigorous approaches to answering their research questions. (p. xv)

It is hoped that this current research study added new knowledge to the research literature, raised awareness of community college presidents and administrators about the impending leadership crisis approaching in the next decade, and provided statistical results that will be of value to community college presidents about perceptions of succession planning for succession leadership in selected community colleges.

Research Questions

The research questions for this research study were:

1. To what extent are selected community colleges in North Carolina preparing future leaders?
2. How are leadership development programs related to succession planning in selected community colleges in North Carolina?
3. How do succession planning strategies consider social, racial, economic and political/cultural nuances for developing leaders in selected North Carolina community colleges?
4. How do research findings show parallels and/or patterns as they are compared to research findings of Lopez-Molina (2008) and Carlson (2007)?

Mixed Methods Design

This current research study was conducted using mixed methods research methodology to collect both quantitative and qualitative data for this research. Creswell (2003) stated that the mixed methods research methodology "adds complexity to a design and uses the advantages of both qualitative and quantitative paradigms. Moreover, the mix methods design best mirrors the research between deductive and inductive models of thinking in a research study" (p. 178). Further, Creswell and Plano Clark (2007) stated that mixed methods research provides "the most complete analysis of problems" (p. 13).

To conduct this current research, this researcher first selected eight community colleges in the state of North Carolina as potential campuses on which to conduct research. The president at each of the selected community colleges was sent a letter (and stamped, self-addressed envelope) from this researcher describing the research and asking for their written permission (on their college letterhead) to conduct research on their campus. The presidents were given the option to either return the permission letter via U.S. mail in the envelope provided or via fax (number was included in initial letter). Each president was also be asked to participate and was sent the Invitation to Participate letter and Consent Form, along with other participants, after this study was approved by Capella University's IRB committee.

Because this researcher had access to the community college employee database which identifies the names and titles of each community college employee, this researcher personally contacted potential participants at each of the eight community colleges. In addition to the president at each of the eight community colleges, this researcher identified other potential participants who are in leadership positions such as vice-president, executive vice-president, executive director, chair and dean. Deans who participated were asked to announce this research study to the Dean's Council in selected North Carolina community colleges. Each potential participant was sent the Invitation to Participate letter and Consent Form. When the Consent Forms were returned from a representative number of potential participants from upper and lower-level tiers of leadership, this researcher instructed SurveyMonkey to send out the Succession Planning Demographics and Participant Survey (Appendix A). SurveyMonkey collected and compiled the data. When the data summary was received from Survey Monkey, this researcher analyzed the data from the surveys. In addition, this researcher placed phone calls to participants who indicated at the end of the survey that they would like to participate in the follow-up interview questions (see Appendix B) either on a face-to-face basis or via phone. Participant surveys that showed that no one had selected to participate in the follow-up interview, this researcher contacted participants via telephone and asked them for a follow-up interview via telephone.

The mixed methods design for this research study was the Triangulation Design: Convergence Model. Creswell and Plano Clark (2007) stated: "This design is used when a researcher wants to directly compare and contrast quantitative statistical results with qualitative findings or to validate or expand quantitative results with qualitative data" (p. 62).

This researcher used the triangulation design and compared and contrasted the results of the qualitative (follow-up interview questions) with quantitative data (participant survey). To expand this research study as a replication research study, this researcher compared and contrasted the results of the previous study of Lopez-Molina (2008) as well as determined and/or strengthened its validity. This is called a convergence model because the quantitative and qualitative data was merged together to reveal provocative information and, hopefully, validated the quantitative research results. The triangulation research design model allowed the researcher to better understand the research results and enhanced the quantitative research findings (see Figure 3). Creswell and Plano Clark (2007) concluded:

> In this model, the researcher collects both types of data within one survey instrument. Because the qualitative items are an add-on to a quantitative survey, the items generally do not result in a rigorous qualitative data set. However, they provide the researcher with interesting quotes that can be used to validate and embellish the quantitative survey findings. (p. 64)

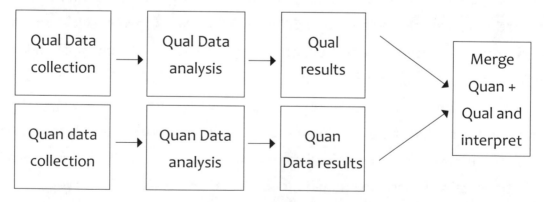

Figure 4. Triangulation Design: Validating Quantitative Data Model

From: *Designing and Conducting Mixed Methods Research*, by J. W. Creswell, and V. L. Plano Clark, 2007, p. 63. Copyright 2007 by Sage. Printed with permission.

Moreover, Lopez-Molina (2008) decided: "To replicate this study, the researcher can apply either the Convergence Model or the Data Transformation Model of the Triangulation Design" (p. 61). This researcher will choose the Convergence Model to determine if qualitative data that will be collected will validate the quantitative data results.

Instrumentation

This research study was a replication/expansion of Lopez-Molina's (2008) study. The instrumentation for this current study was modified versions of the 28-question Survey for Institutional Participants (quantitative data) for administrative participants (see Appendix A) and Follow-up Interview Questions for administrative participants (qualitative data) (see Appendix B) from the Lopez-Molina study.

According to Gall, Gall, and Borg (2003) replication research is the process of repeating a research study with a different group of research participants using the same or similar methods. These authors advocated strongly that the researcher should "seriously consider replicating and extending previous studies rather than trying to investigate a previously unresearched problem" (p. 127). Therefore, this researcher received permission from Dr. Lopez-Molina to use (with modifications to fit the current study) the survey and open-ended interview questions from her 2008 doctoral research study.

Gall, Gall, and Borg stated that constructive replication increases the validity of the theoretical studies in education. According to Lopez-Molina (2008), both her instruments were developed in "corroboration with an external expert and dissertation committee developed both survey instruments and follow-up interview questions used in her initial study (p.65). The outcome of Lopez-Molina's research study showed that higher administrators' perceptions of identifying and preparing future leaders in three selected colleges were not the same as the perceptions of their subordinates who responded. Higher level administrators thought that they were training and preparing future leaders for their institutions, while subordinates at the three institutions thought that future leaders were not being prepared for future leadership roles. Lopez-Molina recommended that her research be expanded to include more community colleges and this resulted in the current study.

Data Collection

To conduct this current research, this researcher first selected eight community colleges in the state of North Carolina as potential campuses on which to conduct research. The president at each of the selected community colleges was sent a letter (and stamped, self-addressed envelope) from this researcher describing the research and asking for their written permission (on their college letterhead) to conduct research on their campus. The presidents were given the option to either return the permission letter via U.S. mail in the envelope provided or via fax (number will be included in initial letter). Each president was also asked to participate and was sent the Invitation to Participate letter and Consent Form, along with other participants, after this study was approved by Capella University's IRB committee.

Because this researcher had access to the community college employee database which identifies the names and titles of each community college employee, this researcher personally contacted potential participants at these eight community colleges. In addition to the president at each of the eight community colleges, this researcher identified other potential participants who are in leadership positions such as vice-president, executive vice-president, executive director, chair and dean. Each potential participant was sent the Invitation to Participate letter and Consent Form. When the Consent Forms had been returned from a representative number of potential participants from upper and lower-level tiers of leadership, this researcher instructed SurveyMonkey to send out the Succession Planning Demographics and Survey for Institutional Participants (Appendix A). SurveyMonkey collected and compiled the data. When the data summary was received from Survey Monkey, this researcher analyzed the data from the surveys. In addition, this researcher placed phone calls to participants who indicated at the end of the survey that they would like to participate in the follow-up interview questions (see Appendix B) either on a face-to-face basis or via phone. Participant surveys that showed no one had selected to participate in the follow-up interview; this researcher contacted participants via telephone and asked them for a follow-up interview via telephone.

Data Analysis

This researcher gave a comprehensive summary of the research results, both qualitative and quantitative. The data analysis of this research study was conducted using the correlation (multivariate) and triangulation (comparative) design, a single-phase timing design which enabled this researcher to collect and analyze quantitative and qualitative data separately, but in tandem (Creswell & Plano Clark, 2007).

After initial data sets of both quantitative and qualitative were categorized, the data was mixed, codified, compared, and correlated and relationships were determined such as leadership development for succession planning. Based on the triangulation design model, this researcher analyzed the quantitative data and analyzed the qualitative data. This researcher drew conclusions and made inferences for the quantitative and qualitative data analysis. Finally, the data analysis was merged into two sets and new findings were declared by asking: Do the data of the two sets converge? How do they converge? Why do they converge? What are the similarities? What are the differences? Is any provocative information revealed? Are there patterns or parallels existing across the analysis? (Creswell & Plano Clark (2007)

Further, this researcher transcribed all taped recorded interviews and analyzed the qualitative data by carefully synthesizing and summarizing the information based on themes and ideas as related to the research questions. Therefore, all supporting data was connected directly to the research questions and, where appropriate, interview responses were provided as evidence of the connection to the research questions.

Ethical Issues

Gall, Gall, and Borg (2003) stated:

An institutional review board (IRB) is a group of individuals who are authorized by an institution to determine whether research studies by colleagues affiliated with the institution comply with institutional regulations, professional standards of conduct and practice and-most critically-the human subjects provisions of the

Code of Federal Regulations for the Protection of Human Subjects. An IRB has at least five members, and their qualifications must satisfy criteria specified in the Federal Code. (Paragraph 46.107) (p. 66).

This researcher received approval from Capella University's Institutional Review Board (IRB) to perform this research study. After approval was received, this researcher submitted an invitation to participate letter. This letter included a "no harms" statement for participating in this research study. In addition, the consent form stated that all information received will be codified so that both the participants and their institutions will be protected and will remain anonymous and all responses will be kept confidential.

Chapter Summary

This current research study was a replication of Lopez-Molina's (2008) study and examined the development of future leaders in selected community colleges in North Carolina. This researcher used the mixed methods research model through the use of a correlation and triangulation design. The instrumentation for this research included both surveys (quantitative) and interviews (qualitative). From the data collected, this researcher identified themes, commonalities, differences, and best practices of leadership development and succession planning in selected community colleges in North Carolina. Research results will be shared with those community colleges that request a copy of this researcher's findings.

CHAPTER 4. DATA COLLECTION AND ANALYSIS

Introduction

The purpose of this study was to examine how eight selected community colleges in North Carolina identified and prepared future leaders. The data collected were examined to determine if the service area demographics and student enrollment ethnicity were reflected in the employees and administration leadership teams within these eight North Carolina community colleges. Special emphasis was made in this research study to examine the strengths and challenges of current leadership development programs and if those programming efforts addressed minority leadership. This study replicated the Lopez-Molina (2008) study by using the participant survey instrument and follow-up interview questions. The survey instrument was modified slightly to fit this study's research sites. The data are presented in this chapter based on each institution's participant response to the online survey and telephone interviews.

A mixed methods research design which combined quantitative (numerical) and qualitative (descriptive) data using surveys and interviews was used. The data collected through the use of close-ended survey questions and open-ended follow-up interview questions were triangulated, compared, and contrasted. Numeric and alpha coding was used to protect the identity of each participant and their institution. Therefore, the alpha codes representing the eight North Carolina community colleges in this study were: A, B, C, D, E, F, G, and H and a numeric code was used for each of the participants at each represented community college as Participant 1, 2, 3 and so on.

This Chapter is organized to 1) display online survey responses and telephone interview results, 2) answer the study's research questions, and 3) lay the foundation for implications, recommendations and conclusions in Chapter 5.

Research Questions

Research questions for this research study are:

1. To what extent are selected community colleges in North Carolina preparing future leaders?

2. How are leadership development programs in North Carolina's selected community colleges related to succession planning for employees?

3. How do succession planning strategies include considerations for social, economic and political/cultural nuances for developing leaders in selected North Carolina community colleges?

4. How do research findings show parallels and/or patterns as they are compared to research findings of Lopez-Molina (2008) and Carlson (2007)?

Descriptive and Demographic Information

In August 2010, eight selected community colleges in North Carolina agreed to participate in this research study. Each president identified a contact person and each contact person identified upper and middle administrators and leaders to respond to the on-line survey. At that time of this research, participants were serving in leadership roles of president, executive vice president, vice president, dean, chair, directors, coordinators, and instructors. All participants were given the opportunity to answer the survey questions and follow-up interview questions.

Overall, a total of 35 participants responded to the online survey and the response rate varied from institution to institution. For example, Institution E had the lowest response rate with only 2 participants (6% of the total responses) while Institution C had the highest response rate with 7 participants (20%) (see Table 1). Fourteen participants (40%) also participated in the follow-up interview. To protect the anonymity of interview participants, they have been coded as P1 through P14. The data classified the participants by their professional title, response rate, and percentage rate (see Table 2).

Six deans and six directors each made up 17% of the participants, for a total of 34% of the participants. Three instructors (9%) participated as well as three chair persons (9%).

Four (11%) presidents and 4 (11%) coordinators participated. A total of 9 (26%) participants were vice presidents.

Table 1. On-Line Survey Participation and Response Rate by Institution Classification

Classification	Rate N=35	Percentage Rate
Institution A	6	17%
Institution B	3	9%
Institution C	7	20%
Institution D	4	11%
Institution E	2	6%
Institution F	6	17%
Institution G	3	9%
Institution H	4	11%
Total 8	N=35	100%

Survey Instruments

The Demographics and Succession Planning Survey (see Appendix A) was applied to eight selected community colleges in North Carolina. The purpose of the survey instrument was to examine how these community colleges developed future leaders and to determine if the leadership and mentoring programs at each institution were reflected in the population demographics in which they served. The survey was divided into two parts. Part I requested personal data for senior administrative participants.

Table 2. Participant Classification by Institution and Title

	Institutions									
Title	A	B	C	D	E	F	G	H	N=35	
President	1	1	1				1		4	11%
Vice President	1	1	1	3		1	1	1	9	26%
Dean	1		1	1		2		1	6	17%
Chair	1		1		1				3	9%
Director			1		1	2		2	6	17%
Coordinator	1	1	2						4	11%
Instructor	1					1	1		3	9%
N=35	6	3	7	4	2	6	3	4	35	100%

Questions 1-6 asked for participant's name, address, telephone number, email address, and institution's name. Part II, Questions 7-28 of the survey instrument requested data on leadership development programs and activities, succession planning, formal and informal mentoring programs, and minority leadership at these eight participating community colleges. Data were requested for the number of years that each participant worked in the community college. With 35 participants reporting, only one participant did not state the number of years of employment. The participants had a combined total of 195 years experience working in these community colleges (see Tables 3 and 4). The highest number of reported working years was 26 and the least amount of working experience reported by participants was one month (see Tables 3 and 4). Participants who worked less than one year and participated in this research made up 17% (6) of the response rate in this research study. A total population of 1,701,298 individuals made up the service areas of these eight institutions.

Follow-up Interview Questions

The purpose of the follow-up interview questions was to collect qualitative data to determine if participants' responses supported the quantitative data results collected from the survey instrument. Fourteen participants (40%) responded to questions from the follow-up interviews via telephone and they answered all the questions.

Table 3. Participants' Title and Years Employed in Upper Leadership Positions

Title	A	B	C	D	E	F	G	H	Total
President	1	1	1	0	0	0	1	0	4
Employed	3yrs 6mos	3yrs 6mos	10yrs				8yrs		
Vice President	1	1	1	3	0	1	1	1	9
Employed	2yrs	4yrs	1yr	26yrs		3 mos.	10yrs	1 mos	
Employed				11yrs					
Employed				7yrs					
Dean	0	0	1	1	0	2	0	1	5
Employed			3 mos.	4yrs		2yrs		3 mos.	
Employed						9yrs			
Chair	2	0	1	0	2	0	0	0	5
Employed	6yrs		1yr						
Employed	6yrs								
Total	4	2	4	4	2	3	2	2	23

Table 4. Participants' Title and Years Employed in Middle and Lower Level Positions

	Institutions								
Title	A	B	C	D	E	F	G	H	Total
Director	0	0	1	0	0	2	0	2	5
Employed			3yrs		4yrs	1yr		3 mos.	
Employed					4yrs	2yrs 9mos		3 mos.	
Coordinator	1	1	2	0	0	0	0	0	4

	5yrs	2yrs	20yrs						
Employed Employed			16yrs						
Instructor Employed	1 10yrs	0	0	0	0	1 3yrs 3mos	1 7yrs	0	3
Total	6	3	7	4	2	6	3	4	35

Data Analysis: Research Question 1

Research Question 1: To what extent are selected community colleges in North Carolina preparing future leaders?

In order to prepare future leaders in community colleges, community college administrators must provide pathways for employees to build leadership competencies before they assume leadership roles in higher education institutions. Professional development pertains to programs that build on the knowledge, skills, and abilities of employees for effective leadership with desired outcomes and expectations.

The survey instrument questions that related to Research Question 1 were questions 10 and 11. Questions 10 asked: Does the community college provide professional development programs or activities for individuals aspiring to assume leadership roles such as president or vice president? Question 11 stated: If you answer "Yes", list the professional development programs or activities and their frequency and if you answer "No", please explain why not. Question 1 of the follow-up interview question related to this research question asked: "What do you consider to be the strengths and challenges of your current leadership development programming efforts?"

Survey data revealed that 29 (83%) participants responded to survey questions 10 and 11 and 6 (17%) skipped the questions. Nineteen (54%) participants stated that leadership development programs are offered at their institution and 10 (29%) participants said that their institution did not offer leadership development programs (see Figure 4).

Participants who stated that their institutions offered leadership development programs named their programs and stated how often the programs were offered. An instructor, A31 wrote: "Yes, the college provides professional development programs or activities for individuals aspiring to assume leadership roles. They offer many leadership classes, mentoring classes, conferences, and so forth as often as they can."

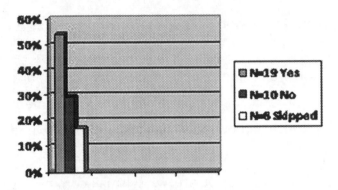

Figure 5. Does your Institution Offer Professional Development Programs?

A vice president (C14) wrote: "Annually professional staff development may apply to North Carolina Community College Leadership Program. Professional Development is provided to faculty and staff two times per year. Also faculty and staff may choose to attend state conferences and leadership training."

A coordinator (B23) and a vice president (D26) identified three professional development programs at their institution and their frequency: Management Best Practices I (FY 2003-2004; FY 2005-2006); Management Best Practices II (Summer 2006); and Management Best Practices III (Summer 2007). Participants did not identify that professional developmental programs were offered after 2007.

Another instructor (F5) wrote that "teaching-learning activities and other professional development opportunities" were offered at their institution on a "monthly" basis.

Participants who listed their leadership development programs and dates revealed that leadership development programs were not offered after 2007. Participants from different community colleges identified the same development activities and practices. The interview response rate to question 1 revealed that participants at Institution F were concerned about a variety of essentials such as size, funding, human resources, communication, and other challenges that they think may have an impact on future leadership development offerings.

Interview Question Responses Related to Question 1

Size of the institution was a concern for one of the community college presidents. He thought that succession planning would be difficult to implement in small community colleges because of the small number of employees. He determined:

> My greatest challenge is that we are a very small community college. My college is very small so that makes Succession Planning very difficult, because you have a relatively small staff. So to be able to identify people is not so concrete simply because there are not so many of people to choose from as there are at the larger institutions (President, C7).

A vice president perceived that because today's community colleges are more complex and are too large to focus on leadership development programs, the challenge to find someone assigned specifically to leadership development building was difficult. He elaborated:

> I think because we are not able to afford having a person with a dedicated focus on leadership development programming. I think that in today's environment there are so many different job responsibilities that are kind of coming to the forefront that are causing the college to not be able to spend as much time on leadership development programs as we would like to put in. So, I think the challenges are having focused personnel and focused program that we could implement and then we could build overtime. (Vice President, F4)

A director thought that leadership opportunities were available at their community college, but employees were too engrossed in their work to receive the messages about leadership development opportunities. Therefore, employees were less informed and only those employees who took time to read the emails could take advantage of the leadership development opportunities. The director explained:

What we have in place I think is pretty organized and pretty encompassing in terms of offering different activities and options for employees to take advantage of probably the biggest challenge is trying to get people informed about the program. Even though you use email to inform people about what's going on across the campus, some people get so bombarded with email that they just really don't pay attention to or don't have time to open up and read every single message that come across their screen. But I would say the college plan is somewhat solid and people who know about it do take advantage of it. (Director, F2)

An English instructor, who also serves on the faculty council and trains other instructors, identified orientation programs as a plus for their institution, but realized that the large part-time employee pool was a challenge to leadership development building. The instructor pointed out:

I believe that we have some good orientation programs. We just have part-time instructors. We have good spring and fall orientations and also on-going training throughout the semester for instructors. One of the weaknesses would be part-time people. Probably one of our biggest challenges is trying to get everyone together as far as doing consolidated training and development with them. (Instructor, F6)

One dean compared current leadership development efforts to former leadership development efforts and noted that leadership development efforts were not currently offered in the community college. However, the dean recognized that leadership development programs "build character and build knowledge" for employees who desire upward mobility. The dean determined:

I think that we do not have a formal leadership development effort. It is more informal-a kind of-as you go progress. You kind of pull yourself along. We do not have formal leadership efforts. We do not have classes. At one time we had a presidential leadership academy and we had a series of classes and that was very helpful, but that's been a long time ago. We don't tend to have that available to us now. Those types of things you know help build character and build knowledge bases for people that are moving up in the agency and we don't currently have that available. (Dean, F1)

One of the president participants pointed out that funding is a challenge that prevents some community colleges from leadership development building. This president also noted that someone (human resources) special, with the right vision, must be a part of a leadership development program's success. He expounded:

Of course there is always that funding issue. Finding funds to effectively get your program off the ground and keep it running and ensure that you have the proper materials as well as experiences for your leadership development program is a challenge. I know that funds are not the only thing that makes your program successful. Secondly, I would say having the right individuals who are basically kind of overseeing running the programs for you. They have to have that vision and carry out the vision as well. So, I think that between the two resources we are talking financial as well as human resources. I would say, thirdly, just communicating the value of leadership across the campus. We've had some pretty good responses from our program. It is pretty good excitement, but it is one of those things that you have to constantly keep before the eyes of your employees. (President, A30)

Participant C12, C13, and H14 stated that they did not know if their institutions implemented leadership development programs.

Data Analysis: Research Question 2

Research question 2: How are leadership development programs in North Carolina's selected community colleges related to succession planning for employees?

Succession planning means identifying and preparing a suitable employee for a position or replacement of an employee in a different role within the organization or institution through job rotation, training and mentoring; e. g. individuals aspiring to lead organizations or institutions. Survey questions 17, 18, 19, 20, 21, and 23 are related to examining succession planning strategies, and how leaders benefit from succession planning offerings at these community colleges.

In order to determine if the succession planning efforts at these community colleges were related to leadership development programs, this researcher first had to determine if there were current succession plans or strategies in place. Survey question 17 asked: Is there a succession plan for administrators at your community college? An overwhelming majority of participants (33 or 94%) either responded negatively (25 or 71%) or skipped the question (8 or 23%) and stated that succession planning was not a part of their institution's leadership development. Only two (6%) participants stated that their institutions offer succession planning for employees. (see Figure 6).

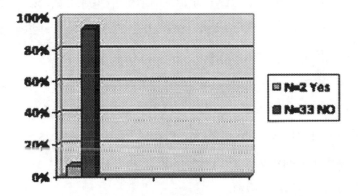

Figure 6.Succession Plans in Selected Institutions

Survey question 18 asked that if participants answered "Yes" to Question 17, then, they were to answer how individuals were indentified and selected to participate in the succession planning process. The survey responses for this question varied:

A vice president (D26) stated: "Employees are supported on their own to develop these skills." A president, (B22) stated that identifying individuals to participate in the succession planning process was "N/A." A dean (H14) stated that he "did not know." Participant A35 (vice-president) stated, "Potential candidates are selected by supervisors and provided guidance."

Survey question 19 asked for the employee classifications that participated in succession planning programs. Twenty-five participants (71%) skipped this question and

10 (29%) answered it, but nine (26%) of the 10 responded "N/A." Only one (3%) participant (A35) responded positively and wrote that "Directors and Coordinators with potential for higher responsibility" were identified and chosen for succession planning programs.

Survey question 20 asked the participants to explain, why their institution did not have succession planning programs. Those who responded to this question answered:

"I am not sure why not. It would be a great way to build morale and grow our own leaders" (Coordinator, A32).

"I don't know of any" (Chair, A33).

"Employees have the flexibility to apply for any position"(Vice president D28).

"Each position is unique. Employees have the opportunity to apply for positions" (Vice president, D27).

Survey question 21 asked: Are your succession planning programs related to leadership development programs at your institution? Please explain the relationship.

Twenty-three participants (66%) answered this question. Twelve participants (34%) skipped the question. Participants wrote:

"Our president looks highly on leadership development which I think is wonderful and everything he does revolves around this" (Instructor, A31).

"Yes, through DCCLD (Developing Community College Leadership) as well as other leadership programs" (Vice president, A35).

"Not that I know of" (Chair, A33).

"We develop leaders, but not through formal succession plans" (Vice president, D 26).

"Yes, leadership programs are designed to prepare employees for higher level positions" (President A30).

"The Institution does not have a Succession Plan" (Coordinator, C8).

"As far as I know they are not" (Director, F5).

"The only succession planning that I am aware of happens within each department. New department chairs are trained, and instructors rotate different subjects to be taught" (Instructor, G25).

Survey question 23 asked: How many of the current senior leaders are graduates of succession planning programs at your institution? The categories identified were president, executive vice president, vice president, dean, and chair. The majority of participants (23 or 66%) identified leaders who they say were graduates of succession planning programs. Twelve participants (34%) skipped the question (see Figure 6).

Participants in this research study identified 14 leaders who benefited from succession planning programs in upper management. Seven (50%) of the leadership group served as Chairpersons. Others who benefited were: President (2 or 13%), Executive Vice President (1 or 15%), Vice President (2 or 13%) and Dean (2 or 13%).

Identifying Future Leaders at Participating Institutions

Survey question 26 asked: How are future leaders identified and selected at your institution to participate in leadership development and succession planning processes?

In this research study, future leaders are individuals who are currently preparing themselves to lead organizations or institutions. Twelve participants (34%) skipped this question, five (14%) stated "I do not know." and 18 participants (51%) responded to this survey question.

One participant remarked: "An application to enroll was required, in letter format, and submitted through the employees' supervisory train." (President, B22)

Another participant (Vice President, A35) explained that leaders are self identified and must demonstrate an interest in leadership development. Other responses included:

"Apply (2020 Vision Committee)." (Vice president, D26)

"Unsure." (Director, H17)

"Depends on the role and job responsibilities." (Vice president, F4)

A director (Director H16) stated that there are two pathways through which leaders are selected: "Performance and degree monitoring. Self projected or brought along by another leader." (Director, H16) A Coordinator participant indicated that the process at this institution was the "Application process" (Coordinator, A32). The majority of the responses was negative, meaning that the participant did not know how leaders were selected.

Survey questions 13, 14, 15, and 16 asked participants if their institution offered mentoring programs and if those mentoring programs were formal or informal. Two (6%) participants skipped this question. Eighteen (51%) participants believed that their institution offered mentoring programs. Conversely, 15 (43%) of participants stated that their institution did not offer mentoring programs (see Figure 4). When participants were asked: "Are your mentoring programs formal or informal" 17(49%) skipped the question. Twelve (34%) reported that the mentoring programs at their institution were formal. Six (17%) reported that their mentoring programs were informal (see Figure 8).

The Interview Responses Related to Research Question 2

Participant responses in this research indicated a mixed understanding of the challenges and strengths of their current leadership mentoring efforts at their institution. For example, responses referred to mentoring programs as having upper management support to mentoring black male students. Participants who expressed a need for having leadership mentoring programs at their institution also pointed out the implications and complexities of implementing mentoring programs at their institution. The follow-up interview question related to Research Question 2 asked: What would you consider to be the strengths and challenges to the existing mentoring efforts of the college?

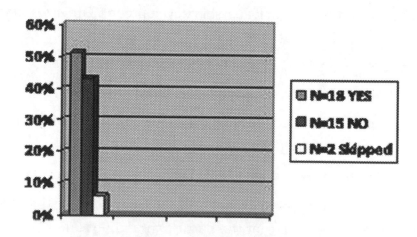

Figure 7. Mentoring Response Rate by Percentage

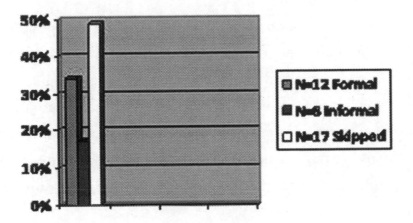

Figure 8. Response by Formal or Informal Leadership Development Programs

The participants responded:

I think the existing mentoring efforts are basically only as strong as the individual that is supplying the mentoring. I think because we have not had a fully developed mentoring program for years that everyone was involved in; I think that we have people who want to help each other who want to help people build their skills, but having the broad base of knowledge and the on-going mentoring program to be able to build on and improve is a challenge. (Vice president, F4)

First of all let me say we have an outstanding leader that leads very strongly in mentoring. I think both of our VPs have bought into that theory. (Director, C10)

I would say, one that we are being pulled in so many directions. Just keeping the focus on mentoring and making sure that individuals receive the attention that they need and given time and because now we are pulled in so many different directions that we just don't have time to give our attention fully to where we need to. So I think that that would be one of the major threats to mentoring. (President, C7)

Well, we had a mentoring program in the past. But we really don't have one right now that is really that active in terms of helping people stay in mid- management are just starting out as directors and department heads or identifying them and helping them think about and work toward achieving higher positions in this college or in another college..I guess some of that may be because of the recession that we have find ourselves in that is somewhat deep may be felt by community colleges for several years into the future which also may have an impact on leadership and advancement possibilities for current employees. More people I think are maybe sacred or just trying to make sure they maintain their current positions instead of going out and searching for other opportunities. (Director, F5)

I really don't know much about them no more than the fact that we have a mentoring program but as far as what is working and what is not the working of the program, I am not privy. I really don't know. I can't honestly say. (Coordinator, C8)

We only have mentoring programs for black males. I wish we had real mentoring programs for leadership improvement within the college to promote our own. (Vice president, H14)

The participants identified time management, the recession, and lack of knowledge of what the mentoring programs have to offer as factors in weak mentoring programs or no mentoring programs. Some indicated the desire to have mentoring programs for employees as well as students.

Follow up Interview Question 2a

This interview question specifically examined if institutions' mentoring efforts included minority candidates. Minority candidates in this research study refer to individuals who are not categorized as unknown or white. It further investigated whether or not cultural nuances were addressed, when minority candidates were selected as leaders in these participating institutions.

Participants did not know if cultural differences were a factor when selecting minorities for leadership positions. Some participants felt that cultural differences should be considered and the response from others indicated that cultural nuances should not be considered. The follow up interview question related to Research Question 2 asked: Are the strengths and challenges the same for minority candidates? If not how are they different?

The participants responded:

Yes, they are exactly the same. (Instructor, F6)

I believe so. I will dare to try to pick them apart; not be the one to start pulling them apart, but no matter what I think these challenges are prevalent and we do need to work on them for the future. (Director, C10)

I think that minority candidates have even more challenges. Especially in that we have fewer minorities as faculty. And I think that often the case is that people-minority candidates mentoring other minority candidates can shed some light on situations that perhaps when you are not a minority candidate working with someone who is very different from themselves they may not always be in tune with some of the issues that a minority faculty member or staff member may deal with. (Vice president, F4)

I think they are. Because I think what I am being asked to do for the current college liaison who is a minority female was the same thing that was done for me and I am not a minority. So, I feel like they are trying to help everybody. They just want the best people. Does that make sense? (Director, F3)

I think it goes along the same way with minority individuals as well as people that are not in the minority area. So I would say it is the same for both. (Instructor, F6)

I think they are basically the same. We make a concerted effort to involve all candidates. We do have a good ratio of minority permanent leadership. In fact, it may even be the opposite here, because we have been so good about making that effort. And I think our minorities do tend to. It is almost like they have within themselves developed a mentoring-ship program to help develop each other, and I don't want to say pull themselves along, but they do tend to help each other learn leadership quality and they do help progress each other along. It is something that I think the Caucasian group is lacking because we do not have a formal plan or formal committee or formal classes. I think that the Caucasians may be less likely to help each other than the minority groups are. I think the minority groups tend to help each other along a little better. (Dean, F1)

For the most part participants who responded to this interview question believed that the challenges for minorities to become leaders were the same as for others. However, some participants raised the issue that minorities do have greater challenges when they are striving to be leaders in community colleges.

Data Analysis: Research Question 3

Research Question 3 asked: How do succession planning strategies include consideration of social, racial, economic and political/cultural nuances for developing leaders in community colleges?

The data collected asked for demographics of the service population including race and ethnicity. Question 3 asked participants to report the number of their population service area. This includes the number of people the institution services in it is county, city, and surrounding community areas. The participants were also asked to provide information on the number of students enrolled, the number of employees at each institution, and the number of administrators at each institution. This information was used to determine racial parity, similarity and racial equality between the service population and enrollment demographics compared to the number of employees and administrators based on their ethnicity representation. The categories that were examined were identified as white, minority, and unknown according to the ethnicity of each individual. (see Table 5 and 6)

According to the data provided by participants (see Table 5 and 6), Institution E had the largest service population (627,846). The student enrollment for institution E was

18,000 in curriculum and continuing education programs with a total of 1,533 employees. Institution B had the largest number of white administrators which made up 91% (20) of the leadership team, while minorities made up 9% (2) of the leadership. The "unknown" was not represented (0). The service area population for Institution B was 215,207.

Institution F reported a service area of 389,000 people. The service area population was comprised of 233,400 white individuals, 93,360 minority individuals, and 62,240 unknown. Student enrollment identified 1,921white students, 2,233 minority students, and 1,263 unknown. The Student enrollment total was 5,417 students. The employment total for Institution F was 331. The total number of white employees reported was 188, minorities were 106, and unknown were 37. Administrators by ethnicity for Institution F were 13 whites, 7 minorities, and 0 unknown. The total number of administrators reported was 20. The percentage of whites in the service area was 60%; minorities were 24%, and unknown were 16%. The percentage rate of whites in enrollment was 35%, minorities was 41%, and unknown were 23%. The white percentage of employees was 57%, minorities were 32%, and unknown were 11%. The white administrators made up 65%, minorities 35%, and 0 unknown.

The percentage of white administrators made up 65% of the total and demonstrated disparity between student enrollment by ethnicity and administrative representation. The 23% unknown enrollment added to 41% minority enrollment rate represented 64% of students enrolled in Institution F. Leadership demographics reported from Institution F indicated that the institution did not achieve racial parity with their service area, their enrollment, in employment, nor in their leadership representation.

A total of 132,306 individuals made up the service area in institution D (89,968 White, 30,430 minorities, and 11,908 unknown). The number of students enrolled in institution D was 4,000 (2,491 Whites, 959 minorities, and 550 unknown. The total number of employees reported was 293 (234 Whites, 50 minorities, and 9 unknown). Total number of administrators reported was 6 (4 Whites, 2 minorities, and 0 unknown). The 100% service area rate reported (68% White, 23% minorities, and 9% unknown). The enrollment rate equaled 100% (62% White, 24% minorities, and 14% unknown). The employee rate equaled 100% (67% Whites, 33% minorities, and 0% unknown). Administrators equaled 100% (67% White, 33% minorities, and 0 unknown). This indicated that Institution D achieved racial parity according to service area, enrollment, and administrators representatives, but did not achieve racial parity in employee representatives. Whites were employed 4 to 1 based on the numbers reported by participants over minorities. Institution D achieved racial parity for unknown in employment, but did not achieve racial parity in administration.

A total of 53, 177 made up the service area for Institution A (38,819 Whites, 13,826 minorities, 532 unknown). The student enrollment was 1,254 (692 Whites, 478 minorities, 84 unknown). The total number of employees was 146 (118 White, 22 minorities, and 6 unknown). Administrators totaled 8 (6 White, 1 minority, and 1 unknown). The service area equaled 100% (73% white, 26% minority, and 1% unknown). The enrollment equaled 100% (55% White, 38% minority, and 7% unknown). The employees equaled 100% (81% White, 15% minorities, and 4% unknown). The administrators equaled 100% (74% White, 13% minorities, and 13% unknown). Institution A achieved racial parity with the white service area and white administrators, but minorities reflect 50% of its leadership team compared to its service population. The unknown leadership team had a higher percentage rate of leadership representation than their service area population and student enrollment.

Institution B service area was 215,207 (160,756 Whites, 10,322 minorities, and 44,129 unknown). The student enrollment was 10,802 (4423 Whites, 4420 minorities, and 1959 unknown). The employees were 696 (564 White, 97 minorities, and 35 unknown). Administrators were 22 (20 White, 2 minorities, and 0 unknown).

Table 5. Institutional Demographics and Percentages by Service Area and Student Enrollment

		College A	College B	College C	College D	College E	College F	College G	College H
	White	38,819	160,756	36,190	89,968	426,935	233,400	37,445	51,527
		73%	75%	55%	68%	68%	60%	29%	58%
	Minority	13,826	10,322	19,082	30,430	125,569	93,360	32,281	36,424
		26%	5%	29%	23%	20%	24%	25%	41%
Service Area	Unknown	532	44,129	10,528	11,908	75,342	62,240	59,397	888
		1%	20%	16%	9%	12%	16%	46%	1%
	Total	53,177	215,207	65,800	132,306	627,846	389,000	129,123	88,839

		100%	100%	100%	100%	100%	100%	100%	100%
	White	692	4,423	823	2,491	12,240	1,921	658	1,712
		55%	41%	51%	62%	68%	35%	28%	43%
	Minority	478	4,420	597	959	3,780	2,233	590	1,161
		38%	41%	37%	24%	21%	41%	25%	29%
Enrollment	Unknown	84	1,959	193	550	1,980	1,263	1,110	1,127
		7%	18%	12%	14%	11%	23%	47%	28%
	Total	1,254	10,802	1,613	4,000	18,000	5,417	2,358	4,000
		100%	100%	100%	100%	100%	100%	100%	100%

The service area equaled 100% (75% White, 5% minorities, and 20% unknown). Enrollment equaled 100% (41% White, 41% minorities, and 18% unknown).

Employees equaled 100% (81% White, 14% minorities, 5% unknown). Administrators equaled 100% (White 91%, 9% minorities, and 0% Unknown). Racial parity in institution B is lacking with unknown and minorities. The unknown and minorities make up 59% of student enrollment but show 9% of the leadership team.

Institution C service area was 65,800 (36,190 Whites, 19,082 minorities, and 10,528 unknown). Enrollment was 1,613 (823 White, 597 minorities, and 193 unknown). Employees were 132 (103 White, 26 minorities, and 3 unknown. Administrators were 10 (10 White, 0 minorities, and 0 unknown). The service area equaled 100% (55% White, 29% minorities, 16% unknown). Enrollment equaled 100% (51% White, 37% minority, and 12% unknown).

Table 6. Institutional Demographics and Percentages by Employees and Administrators

	A	B	C	D	E	F	G	H
White	118	564	103	234	1,364	188	166	206
	81%	81%	78%	80%	89%	57%	60%	90%
Minority	22	97	26	50	153	106	52	18
	15%	14%	20%	17%	10%	32%	19%	8%

Employees	Unknown	6	35	3	9	16	37	58	5
		4%	5%	2%	3%	1%	11%	21%	2%
	Total	146	696	132	293	1,533	331	276	229
		100%	100%	100%	100%	100%	100%	100%	100%
	White	6	20	10	4	7	13	8	9
		74%	91%	100%	67%	78%	65%	57%	100%
	Minority	1	2	0	2	2	7	4	0
		13%	9%	0%	33%	22%	35%	29%	0%
Administrators	Unknown	1	0	0	0	0	0	2	0
		13%	0%	0%	0%	0%	0%	14%	0%
	Total	8	22	10	6	9	20	14	9
		100%	100%	100%	100%	100%	100%	100%	100%

Employees equaled 100% (78% White, 20% minorities, and 2% unknown). Administrators equaled 100% (100% White, 0% minorities, and 0 percent unknown). In Institution C, minority and unknown service area population and student enrollment had 0% representation and are not reflected in the Administrative team and are lacking racial parity.

Institution G service area was 129,123 (37,445 Whites, 32,281 minorities, and 59,397 unknown). The student enrollment was 2,358 (658 Whites, 590 minorities, and 1,110 unknown). Employees were 276 (166 Whites, 52 minorities, 58 unknown). Administrators were 14 (8 Whites, 4 minorities, 2 unknown). Service area equaled 100% (29% White, 25% minorities, and 46% unknown). Enrollment equaled 100% (28% White, 25% minorities, and 47% unknown). Employees equaled 100% (60% White, 19% minorities, and 21% unknown). Administrators equaled 100% (57% White, 29% minorities, and 14% unknown).

Institution G, unknown groups were underrepresented in leadership teams and in employee representation. The unknown made up 46% of the service area population and 47% of the enrollment, but was reflected in employment as 21% of employees and 14% of administrators. Institution G demonstrated inequality for the unknown in administrators and employees representation.

Institution H service area was 88,839 (51,527 White, 36,424 minorities, and 888 unknown). Enrollment was 4,000 (1,712 White, 1,161 minorities, and 1,127 unknown). The employees were 229 (206 White, 18 minorities, 5 unknown). Administrators were 9 (9 White, 0 minorities, and 0 unknown). The service area equaled 100% (58% White, 41% minorities, and 1% unknown). Enrollment equaled 100% (43% White, 29% minorities, and 28% unknown). Employees equaled 100% (90% White, 8% minorities, and 2% unknown). Administrators equaled 100% (100% White, 0% minorities, and 0% unknown). Institution H student enrollment of minorities and unknown were 57%; whereas, there leadership team representation was 0%.

The institutional demographics according to percentages for Institutions A, B, C, D, E, F, G and are combined in Tables 5 and 6.

This research study was conducted to examine how community colleges include minority leadership and diversity at their institutions. Racial parity is achieved when employees and administrators percentage representation is equaled in comparison to percentage rate representation of service area population and student enrollment. The demographics data collected demonstrated racial parity in some areas and inequality in other areas.

Table 7 showed the combined demographics for eight community colleges in North Carolina researched in this current study. The entire service area totaled 1,701,298 (1,075,040 Whites (63%); 361,294 minorities (21%); and 264,964 (16%) unknown). Student enrollment was 47,444 (24,962 White (53%); 14,218 minorities (30%); and 8,266 (17%) unknown).

Table 7. Eight Selected Community Colleges Combined Demographics and Percentages

Service Area	White	1,075,040	63%
	Minority	361,294	21%
	Unknown	264,964	16%
	Total	1,701,298	100%
Enrollment	White	24,962	53%
	Minority	14,218	30%
	Unknown	8,266	17%
	Total	47,444	100%
Employees	White	2,943	81%
	Minority	524	14%
	Unknown	169	5%
	Total	3,636	100%

	White	77	79%
Administrators	Minority	18	18%
	Unknown	3	3%
	Total	98	100%

Employees totaled 3,636 (2,943 Whites (81%); 524 minorities (14%); and 169 (5%) unknown). Administrators combined total was 98 (77 White (79%), 18 minorities (18%); and 3 (3%) unknown). The combined total and percentage rate demonstrated that the enrollment was 53% White, 30% minorities and 17% unknown. The administrative teams and employee teams demonstrated that minorities and unknowns could be added to reflect the 47% of student enrollment.

This research study examined how community colleges offer pathways for upward mobility to employees within and across classifications. Survey Question 7 asked:

Upon hiring new employees, does the community college offer pathways for upward mobility within and across classifications (pathways in succession planning to senior level positions through formal and informal mentoring programs)?

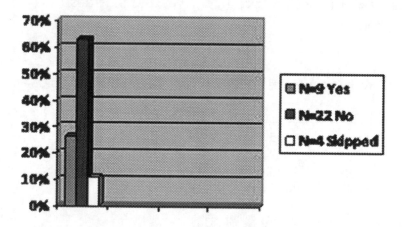

Figure 9. Pathways of Upward Mobility

Of the 35 participants, 31(89%) answered this question and 4 (11%) skipped it. Nine (26%) stated "Yes," their institution offered pathways for upward mobility, but 22 (63%)

answered "No," their institution does not offer pathways to upward mobility to inspiring leaders.

Participants were given an opportunity to provide reasons their institutions did not offer pathways of upward mobility and describe the hiring process. The participants did not define or describe specific programs that trained new employees or offered new employees opportunities for upward mobility. The participants explained:

"Either by recognition to promotion or through application and additional credentials." (Vice president, H14)

"Can't say yes in terms of a program, but I feel I learned a great deal from the former Chair, informally. However, I wasn't groomed for the job." (Chair C11)

"I don't know." (Coordinator C12)

"I was encouraged to attend training and workshops to broaden my knowledge base." (Director, H17)

"No, however, we are working on this concept at this time and intend to have a good program in place within the next 12 months." (Vice president B21)

"Do not have a mentoring program in place for administrators." (Vice president, F4)

"The only leadership development program that I am aware that includes minority populations happens between students and faculty members. We have an instructor who leads minority black males in a program on campus." (Instructor, G25)

"N/A" (Dean, C13).

"The selection process reviews the diversity of applicants." (President, A30)

"The College employee's minority applicants as often as possible, if qualified." (President, G24)

"Diversity is always a consideration-Race/Gender." (Vice president, H14)

"We have plenty of minority leaders, but no program." (Chair, C11)

Follow-up Interview Question 2b

Follow-up Interview Question 2b asked: How are cultural nuances addressed when mentoring minority candidates?

This interview question further investigated whether or not cultural nuances were addressed, when minority candidates were selected as leaders in these participating institutions. In some cases, participants understood the meaning of not making differences when selecting minority candidates, but were not sure as to whether or not cultural nuances was a factor that should or should not be considered. Some participants felt that cultural differences should be considered and responses from others indicated that cultural nuances should not be considered.

A vice president stated that people, in general, do not appreciate or understand diversity and that we all should understand that we are not from the same "cookie cutter." He stated:

> I think that we understand and appreciate diversity to an extent that is very positive. No one can fully walk in another person's shoes but I do think that we do really appreciate diversity. I think that part of it is being in the region that we are in. I think that we often think about diversity though being racial, ethnic, religious those types of things. I think we often have to remind each other that appreciating diversity is appreciating true diversity we do not have to have to all think things through the same way we don't have to have the same mindset. We don't have to have the same way we would interact with people. We need to appreciate all aspect of people's diversity and not expect us all to be cookie cutter out of the same mole kind of folks. (Vice President, F4)

A president compassionately explained the reason minorities need extra mentoring and "additional development." He explained his rationale for the need of minorities to be equipped to maneuver around barriers that are sometimes challenges for minorities and females. He rationalized:

> I think that with minority candidates you have some additional mentoring work to do some additional development and I don't mean that in a negative way. I just mean that sometimes minorities live in what I call two different worlds. They live in the minority world and as well as the majority world. I think part of this is learning how to negotiate in both and be successful in developing leadership

skills. I think that is the additional mentoring- the additional development that is needed. Again, like I say, it is not a negative it just the reality of being a member of a minority group. The same thing applies with females. As you know they also have to navigate being female as well as having to navigate entering into leadership positions. They have to know how to overcome some of the barriers that may be there. I think that those are part of your leadership development. Sometimes those barriers will not be removed, but how do you navigate around those barriers. So I think that's the additional need there. (President, C7)

One of the directors was wrestling with his thoughts about cultural nuances in the community college and found it very difficult to respond to the question. He showed his doubt by stating:

I am not sure they are. I'm not really sure that cultural nuance is dealt with very effectively. And I think that it is because there are so many variations of culture and that just so much goes into culture as there are so many differences. So it's one that is very tough to really even address. I really just don't think. I think there needs to be quite a bit more work in that particular area. (Director, F5)

Surprisingly, a dean stated this as a response:

"I feel that I am at a little disadvantage as an outsider looking in" (Dean, C13).

One of the directors had an insight for individual nuances when dealing with all people in work relations, but recognized that there is not a quick fix as to how cultural nuances should be addressed when mentoring minorities. The director concluded:

I think it is important to understand the people who are in front of you who are sitting there being counseled and being guided by you. I think it is important to understand their background and the challenges that they face. I think each group is different. It depends on the clientele that you are counseling or mentoring. I don't know if there is a silver bullet for any particular minority group rather than understand that they are individually different and each has knowledge that you have to work toward. (Director, C10)

An instructor demonstrated in her answer on how difficult it is to address cultural nuances in the community college where she works. From the instructor's point of view, cultural nuances are overlooked intentionally. The instructor generalized:

I really don't know if I can really answer that question or not. I think they are dressed in terms of being sensitive to people's religions and political affiliations and that kind of thing, but if that is addressed if you are talking about matching up people that are the same as mentoring someone else that is the same, I don't see that we are going into that detail around here. (Instructor, F6)

In contrast to this instructor above, one of the deans pointed out:

I think we are aware of minorities. We are sensitive to their needs and understand that they are a part of our student body and a part of our communities. We make a conscience effort to hire minorities. (Dean, F1)

Future Topics for Further Study in Developing Minority Leaders

Identifying minority leadership in community colleges was one aspect of this research study. Participants were asked to identify topics that they thought should be addressed when hiring minorities as future leaders.

Follow-up interview question 3 related to Survey Question 3 and asked: What topics do you foresee needing further study in developing leaders of minority populations? When asked to present topics that needed further study in developing minority populations, many of the participants could not find topics to share. Conversely, others were willing to share topics and offer recommendations for future minority leaders. One instructor stated that the institution is not addressing minority leadership going forward. She speculated:

Leaders should be developed from within community colleges. This would be good to do. I do believe that our Human Resources department is actually working on that. They have actually implemented a leadership program just recently. I don't know that it addresses minorities specifically. I think it includes everyone. (Instructor, F6)

One of the deans cited "communication" as a topic that should be considered by aspiring minority leaders. This dean declared:

I think sometimes communications. I really think that is about it. Because I think they do very well as far as getting in school. I think they do very well with finding monies to go back to school and complete their education but other than that, networking and finding the group they net work with, and once they get on board,

I mean they do an excellent job. I find that people that I have worked with who do have opportunities to go back to school to further their education that it does not seem to be a stumbling block whatsoever. (Dean, F1)

For one director, student retention rate was the main topic for everyone going forward.

The director stated:

One of the things that is the focus for not only just minority leaders but leaders across the board is trying to increase the retention rate of students across the board. Getting them to really focus on why they are here and the importance of doing well here on this level at the community college and because of the doors it will open up later in life for them. (Director, F5)

A dean pointed out that "cultural nuances" is the topic to address and this topic even provoked her to assess training that she gave to a minority at the community college. She pointed out:

Maybe the cultural nuances you just mentioned. It makes me think. Am I giving her all the information that she needs? Is there something that I know that she doesn't know? Because I always say that- If you know you don't know it you can ask about it. But if you are completely unaware that you don't know-you know what I mean- So I think that would be the thing; Is that I would hope that I am doing the best job for her that I can. But is there something that I don't even know that I should be talking to her about that she doesn't know to ask me about. So training on that would great, I think. (Dean, F2)

One of the vice president painted a diversity picture by pointing out all the different nationalities that are enrolled in the community college. This vice-president stated that diversity has grown at the community college and that diversity in minority leadership should be taken into account. He assessed the situation thusly:

I think understanding the true mission and role of community colleges past and present is important. I think understanding budget implications; understanding many people here have a very narrow view because it's a world around them. When community colleges serve so many different people of different ages, different education needs, different training needs, coming from so many socioeconomic situations that I think helping everyone is needed and especially minorities, Especially here we have students from over 100 different countries in our credit programs- not talking about English as a second language; not talking about continuing education, English classes or foreign language classes, but we are talking about in our credit programs students from over 100 different countries. And so, we really need to teach an appreciation of diversity in so many ways on so many levels but starting and beginning with real communication such as those interpersonal communications, email communications, communication between supervisors and employees, among supervisors and, I mean at every level. (Vice president, F4)

An instructor stated:

Maybe leadership should be to develop leaders from within would probably be a good one. And I think that I do believe that our HR department is actually working on that. They've actually implemented a program just recently a leadership program, I don't know that it addresses minorities specifically, I think it includes everyone. (Instructor, F6)

A director shared that minorities should understand the role of the community college going forward and that the role of the community college is to mentor minorities and train them so they can succeed: The director said:

Understanding the community college system in general; I think that so many times we get that leadership training once we arrive at a particular position. I'm afraid that we don't do a good job at the community college in grooming people along the way. I think sometimes we get to where we want to be, but don't know how we got there. I think in order to be our very best, we are going to have to go start going back to the intermediate level and provide the same mentoring and training. For instant a lot of time you work hard and may get to several administrative positions in the institution. But the true training and guidance there needs to be an intermediate level of leadership programs that will be shared as we climb to various positions that we want. I am not so sure that those programs are in play. (Director, C10)

A president offered several topics for aspiring minorities to be aware of in the future, such as budgeting, globalization, and human resources. The president offered the following statement:

Further topics; I would probably venture to say "global issues". Be aware of the global society that we live in. Of course that is for everybody. But, I think even a minority candidate need to be very aware of how our society interacts on a global state. I would also say part of being successful as minorities in leadership position is the development of budgeting and financial skills as well as-just making sure that when you are in charge of a large enterprise that you also know what the fiscal responsibilities are for leaders. Third, I would also say we are coming into a society now where the media is everywhere officially and unofficially you may be on U-tube one day and the big tube the next and you really need to know how to manage your presence in various media. I think that is going to be a very important area to be successful. I think those are three things being globally aware, having a fiscal understanding and background if you can gain some actual budgeting financial resource allocation experience and again dealing with the media because you never know when you are going to be approached by the media. So those are areas that I think are increasing more. And If I had to add another one probably human resources because you are going to be leading people and how do you work with that-even though I know most folks say well I have a human resource director but you still have to understand the ins and outs of human resources and how to administer Human resource programs. (President C7)

Data Analysis: Research Question 4

The literature review revealed that very little research was done in the area of succession planning and succession leadership in community colleges or in higher education (AAWCC, 2006). Research question 4 asked: How do research findings show parallels and/or patterns as they are compared to research findings of Lopez-Molina (2008) and Carlson (2007)?

The literature review forecasted that an impending leadership crisis is facing higher education leadership due to baby boomer's retiring (Lopez-Molina, 2008, Carlson, 2007). The American Association of Community Colleges and others have warned higher education about this leadership crisis as far back as 2006. In 2007, Carlson conducted a study that investigated how Colorado community colleges identified and prepared future leaders. In 2008, Lopez-Molina conducted a study that examined how three community colleges were developing future leaders.

Lopez-Molina's (2008) study further raised the issue of how the three community colleges addressed minority leadership, mentoring programs, and if the demographics of the service area were reflected in student enrollment and administrative teams. This current research study (2011) replicated Lopez-Molina's (2008) study and investigated how eight community colleges in North Carolina prepare future leaders and specifically analyzed if those eight community colleges achieved racial parity. Racial parity is achieved when service area ethnicity and student enrollment ethnicity is reflected with equity in administrative and employee teams.

Lopez-Molina's (2008) study revealed that the three community colleges that she investigated were located in diverse areas of the United States (Florida, Ohio, and Texas).

Carlson's (2007) study confined her investigative research to 13 community colleges in Colorado. This current research study investigated eight community colleges in North Carolina.

Carlson's (2007) study did not address race or ethnicity as part of her research study as did Lopez-Molina's study and this current study. But Carlson's (2007) found that Colorado community colleges "need to identify and prepare future leaders in their institutions and succession plans should incorporate both system and college needs." (p. 140). Carlson (2007) raised the issue of succession planning and identified five components of a succession leadership program as follows:

> This recommendation includes a five-part succession leadership program for the Colorado Community College system. The five components consist of an individual career development plan to indentify skill gap analysis, internships, experience, mentoring, feedback, and exposure to higher levels of leadership within the system. (p. 135)

Neither the Lopez-Molina (2008) study nor this research study recommended a specific type of succession plan or components. But what the Lopez-Molina's (2008) study and this current study did was to raise the issue of racial parity. Both Carlson (2007) and Lopez-Molina (2008) contributed to the literature of higher educational leadership and recommendation for further study that guided this current research study.

Chapter Summary

Chapter 4 reported data collected from a survey instrument and follow-up interviews for this research study. The chapter was organized to demonstrate the answers to the research questions based on data collected from the survey instrument and the follow-up interview responses. The purpose of this chapter was to present data that would determine how eight community colleges were preparing future leaders and if those community colleges achieved racial parity. The data results were contrasted and compared to research findings in Carlson (2007) and Lopez-Molina (2008) research studies. Furthermore, the data from this chapter will be used for conclusions, implications, and recommendations in Chapter 5.

CHAPTER 5. RESULTS, CONCLUSIONS, AND RECOMMENDATIONS

Introduction

Research studies demonstrated that community colleges are facing a potential leadership crisis because of the need to replace baby boomers who are reaching retirement age (Jamilah, 2006; Wolverton, 1999; Cohen & Brawer, 2002). Moreover, Duree's (2008) study documented that the number of community college leadership program graduates decreased by 78% from 1983 to 1997. Duree (2008) warns in his research that

> If you think about that time period, those would be the people who would really be in the chute to take the place of those who were retiring. So actually, not only is there the anticipated exodus going out the door, but there also is a shortage of qualified candidates coming in. (p. 1)

North Carolina is home to the third largest community college system in the United States and has 58 community colleges located throughout the state. When President Lancaster retired from the North Carolina Community College System office in 2007, he perceived that the community college system would be facing massive retirements and possible leadership gaps within some of the system's institutions. He noted that 59 presidents, 54 senior administrators, 48 faculty, and 48 staff members were eligible for retirement. He concluded that the North Carolina Community College System would need trained and qualified leaders to replace potential retirees between 2010 and 2014. This laid the foundation for this research study.

This current research study replicated Lopez-Molina's (2008) research study that surveyed three colleges in three different states to determine how they were preparing future leaders. This research study expanded Lopez-Molina's (2008) research to eight community colleges in North Carolina. These eight community colleges were investigated to determine how they prepare future leaders. The survey instrument and follow-up interview questions used in this current research study were from Lopez-Molina's (2008) research study, but were modified slightly to fit the parameters of this study.

The data collected and interviews conducted were examined and presented in Chapter 4. Chapter 5 is organized to 1) present an overview of implications from the results of the research questions; 2) show common themes between the Lopez-Molina (2008) and Carlson (2007) studies, and this current research study; and 3) offer recommendations for future research.

Implications from Research Questions

Research Question 1

The first research question in this study asked to what extent are leadership development programs offered at the community colleges for employees aspiring to assume leadership roles in higher education institutions. Of the eight selected community colleges in North Carolina, only one (13%) offered development programs. Notwithstanding, these eight community colleges offered opportunities annually for employees to attend state and national leadership development conferences, local workshops and leadership activities. Some participants identified Leadership Academy, Future Vice President Leadership, and Community College Leadership as leadership development opportunities for individuals interested in improving their leadership skills and becoming better leaders. Other participants did not know what, or if, any leadership opportunities were available or offered at their institution.

When participants were asked if their leadership development programs were formal or informal, most reported that they did not have a formal leadership development program but that informal leadership mentoring was provided either by another leader at the community college or individuals were on their own to learn about new leadership positions. Thus, this research showed that informal training within these eight community colleges was offered to potential leaders but that, in most cases, formal leadership development opportunities were lacking.

Lopez-Molina (2008) found that there was some upward leadership mobility and of the three colleges she studied, some of the participants acknowledged that leadership development programs were realized, while others acknowledged that upward mobility pathways were not apparent and that visible pathways to leadership succession was not present at their institution. One individual in Lopez-Molina's (2008) study specifically noted:

> Our college has an extensive leadership program that allows a cohort of leadership candidates to gain critical leadership training. The College has promoted several of the graduates of this program to advanced administrative positions. (Lopez-Molina, p. 78)

Conversely, another participant stated:

> This college does not appear to have a visible pathway to higher level positions. The college does not restrict access necessarily either but upward moves have the appearance of being more informal than by design. Many positions have no identifiable 'next step' and often they become an upper limit. Lateral moves are not uncommon but there does not appear to be a formal means to upper administrative positions. The culture is almost a 'by invitation only' atmosphere. (Lopez-Molina, p. 79)

In Carlson's (2007) study, participants noted that encouragement was given to those individual who were interested in participating in leadership development training. Some of her participants noted that lateral transfers were made within or between divisions to give individuals different work or developmental experiences and they were encouraged to attend state and national leadership development training.

Research Questions 2

In research Question 2 the participants were asked: How are leadership development programs related to succession planning in the community college for employees?

This question elicited responses that ranged from individuals not knowing if their college provided leadership development programs, to individuals stating emphatically that their institutions discussed the importance of leadership development with very little effort of providing the opportunities for employees that related to succession planning.

In the Lopez-Molina (2008) study, one participant stated:

> These two areas are disconnected at this college. We have lots of talk about leadership and new leadership topics from books and other sources. But the interest in leadership is primarily so that we can perform at an optimal level in our current positions. It does not appear to be designed to help most of us move up either at this institution or any other per se. Leadership development also appears to exempt upper level administration. They spend a great deal of time talking about the importance of leadership and its positive benefits but they spend very little time actually practicing the activities themselves. (Participant 6, p. 79)

In this current study, participants revealed that the president of the institution decided who the next potential leaders were going to have the opportunity to attend the President's Leadership Seminar. Employees were given the opportunity to submit applications to attend the President's Leadership Seminar program and the president screened the candidates and announced the chosen one. Conversely, in the Carlson (2007) study, one participant stated that "preparing for succession of leadership at their institution was part of the college's overall plan" (p. 110).

Carlson (2008) concluded that the majority of respondents disagreed with the statement that their institution's leadership development programs related to succession planning.

Hence, the majority of participants in all three research studies stated that their institution leadership development programs, if they existed, did not relate to succession leadership planning nor were they designed to train their future leaders for promotion from within.

Research Question 3

Research question 3 asked: How do succession planning strategies include considerations for social, racial, economic and political/cultural nuances for developing leaders in the community college? In 2007, Carlson's study revealed that minority leadership was not a focus in her research study. Conversely, Lopez-Molina's (2008) study targeted minority leadership and the nuances of culture. This current research study replicated Lopez-Molina's (2008) study and found that the results were similar.

Lopez-Molina's (2008) participants stated: "Since the Hispanic community will experience tremendous growth and become a majority in the Southern U. S., it is paramount that institutions seriously consider developing presidential succession strategies that are focused towards minorities, especially Latinos" (p. 81). Another participant statement from the Lopez-Molina study regarding cultural nuances was "I am not sure the cultural nuances are addressed" (p. 81). In this current research study, a statement was made by one participant that was similar to this statement. Participant 8, coordinator in Institution C, stated: "I am not sure they are. I am not sure that cultural nuances are dealt with very effectively." Carlson's (2007) study did not mention racial minorities or racial parity concerning demographic service area populations and student enrollment being reflected in administrative and employment teams.

Research Question 4

How does Carlson's (2007) study and Lopez-Molina's (2008) study compare to this current research study?

The results from this current study revealed that potential leaders who work in community colleges would like succession planning that is realistic and is geared toward higher leadership positions within the community colleges. Participants in this research study in each institution expressed the desire to have succession plans for promotions, career development, and upward leadership mobility.

In some cases, administrators demonstrated that they had no desire to implement succession plans for leadership upward mobility and felt that state, national, and local conferences provided employees with the proper training. Conversely, other community colleges presidents are interested in succession planning for potential leaders and have already begun implementation.

All three research studies revealed that succession planning in community colleges is a topic that has been brought to the forefront. In fact, since Carlson's (2007) study, the topic of leadership development through succession planning has grown. This current research study revealed that some community colleges have already begun to incorporate leadership development with emphasis on preparing future leaders through succession planning within the community college (see Table 8).

Table 8. Analogous Research Findings

Topics	Smith 2011	Molina-Lopez 2008	Carlson 2007
Colleges are preparing future leaders	Very little	Very little	No
Are succession planning strategies used in identifying and training future leaders	Very little	Very little	No
Minorities are included in future leadership positions	Some	Very little 2.00%	Not mentioned at all 0.0%
Student enrollment and service area population are reflected in leadership teams	In some areas	No	No
Are selected community colleges prepared for leadership crisis	No	No	No
Are upper leaders interested in leadership succession			

planning	No	No	No
Are employees interested in succession leadership	Yes	Yes	Yes

This current research study also revealed a dichotomy of thought among senior-level leaders in the eight community colleges. For the most part, administrators believe that the leadership development programs offered at the state and national level are enough to develop future leaders. Other presidents are aware of the importance of leadership development programs for succession, but their budgets do not have the funds and human resources to develop such programs. Most of the participants in this research study felt that in order to develop succession planning for potential leaders, the president of the institution would have to be the guiding source behind succession planning for future leadership within the institution. Middle management supported having professional development programs at their institution. Although succession planning for future leaders is growing at a slow pace, the trend toward racial parity between demographics and student enrollment to reflect leadership teams is growing. Lopez-Molina (2008) found a disparity between demographics service area, student enrollment, and leadership teams. She stated:

> It is my contention that these institutional demographics suggest that the needs and the opportunities do, indeed, exist to strategically address increasing enrollment and employment that is more reflective of their minority populations as a way of responding to the minority leadership disparity in the community college environment. (p. 89)

Of the eight community college examined in this research study, 6 (75%) showed some racial parity in certain areas. Community college F showed a lack of racial parity in all areas and community college H showed no minority representation in leadership teams. In community college B, minority enrollment was 41% but minority participation on leadership teams was only 9%.

In all three research studies, a succession leadership model is very important for the community college system as a whole; but, more importantly, for the individual community college employees. Carlson (2007) stated that a formalized succession plan should be implemented to ensure the improvement of each college's most valuable resource, its employees.

In order for community colleges to remain unique institutions that prepare future employees for labor markets, its leaders must examine its culture, implement additional strategies for cultural change that include global representation of diverse ethnicities, and begin to develop and implement programs to prepare future leaders. Community college leaders of the future must be knowledgeable enough to change the culture of the community college to include different cultures and diversity. Participants in this current research study identified topics for community college leaders to consider going-forward. They are:

1. Prepare leaders who see "community" as a global market.
2. Prepare leaders to invest in their employees to help develop them for global leadership
3. Change the culture of the community college to reflect globalization.
4. Invest in community college employees and prepare them to be knowledgeable, fiscal responsible and creative thinkers.
5. Develop succession plans that offer employees a realistic opportunity for upward mobility.
6. Offer mentoring to aspiring leaders who desire up-ward mobility within the community college system.
7. Research leadership succession plan models and choose to invest in human resources.

Lopez-Molina (2008) stated:

> In order for community colleges to be strategically positioned to address the projected shortage of the prepared leaders, the current leadership must proactively address the need and the development of a comprehensive and integrative leadership development program and succession plan that includes mentoring. Community colleges must address the racial and ethnic disparity

amongst individuals identified to assume the leadership roles. They must consider an emphasis on developing minority leaders as a critical element in creating leaders representative of the student population, service area, and the employees. (AACC, 2002, 2005, 2006: U.S. Census, 2007, p. 95)

Recommendations

This study investigated how eight community colleges in North Carolina are preparing future leaders. It also examined if the service area population and student enrollment were reflected in the employee and leadership teams. Based on the results of this research study, the following recommendations are presented to leaders in community colleges:

1. Expand the role of the community college's mission by investing in its human resources and extending the mission to reflect a global community.
2. Evaluate employees in community colleges and identify those potential leaders who desire upward mobility leadership and provide realistic opportunities for promotions.
3. Examine leadership development programs that relate to succession plans in other community colleges and develop a plan at your own institution.
4. Invest in community college employees and offer opportunities for job shadowing, leadership skills building and support career development.
5. Expand the vision to include leadership teams that support employees.
6. Collaborate with state community college system leaders and ask for guidance in developing leadership development programs and succession planning.
7. Collaborate with national organizations and search for national programs that will support local efforts to develop comprehensive leadership development programs, succession planning, and leadership mentoring programs.
8. Provide opportunities for employees who are current leaders to train and learn the job skills for the next leadership level before it becomes vacant.

9. Survey subordinates to determine if they are interested in building leadership skills through succession planning

10. Support emerging leaders within community colleges and reflect the demographics of the service area populations.

11. Evaluate the community college hiring practices and implement hiring practices that are ethical and inclusive, reflecting loyalty within the ranks served.

12. Consider racial, ethnic, and cultural nuances within the mission, vision, and values of the community college.

13. Conduct research to determine best practices of leadership development models in community colleges and business.

14. Promote and include diversity in leadership teams and develop future leaders.

15. Invest in human resources, community colleges employees, by providing leadership training opportunities to current mangers for upper leadership positions.

Suggestions for Further Research

Based on the research findings in this current research study, the topics for future research are offered:

1. Conduct a case study to compare leadership development programs that are being implemented in community colleges.

2. Examine leadership development plans in businesses, colleges, and community colleges and determine if minorities are considered within these plans.

3. Develop a Leadership Development Model that would reflect consideration for minorities, nationals, and with an emphasis of global representation on leadership teams

4. Expand this research study to include more community colleges.

5. Conduct a research study to determine how community colleges are using their own human resources to develop future leaders.

6. Conduct a research study to include only minorities to determine how they see themselves as it relates to succession planning and leadership development in their community college.

7. Conduct a study of presidents in community college and determine the characteristic of presidents who provide leadership development programs and succession planning and share the information with community college systems.

Chapter Summary

Based on research findings, the community college system in each state must be the harbinger to support, promote, and encourage local community colleges to implement leadership development programs that reflect local and global nationals. Local community colleges must develop strategies to achieve parity within their service area. Employment opportunities must be continued after employees receive full-time positions and leadership development programs instituted to develop leaders who are knowledgeable, creative, and possess leadership competencies.

Since Joliet Junior College was founded in 1901, the community college has served as a refuge for those seeking improvement in education, job skills, and economic development. This "lighthouse" in the community college should not grow dim but, rather, should grow brighter. To brighten the flame community college systems must be the catalyst to introduce community college upper leadership to the idea of leadership development related to succession planning. Equal opportunities must be presented that represent equal employment with minority inclusion through leadership development programs and succession planning. As community colleges continue to evolve in the United States, the leadership in community colleges must demonstrate an understanding of change, economic growth, and globalization. The American Association of Community Colleges stated:

Globalization is driving changes in our economy, and the need for an educated workforce has never been greater. The majority of new jobs that will be created by 2014 will require some postsecondary education. In addition, the demographics of the workforce are changing. As a result, employers increasingly rely on the very students who currently are least likely to complete their education. (para. 3)

Most importantly, it is community college leaders who must make the difference and strengthen the purpose of the community college by demonstrating leadership competencies that implement leadership development programs for succession planning and prepare competent leaders, including minorities, who will keep the lighthouse in the community college shining for many to enter therein in the future.

REFERENCES

Abelman, R., & Dalessandero, A. (2008). The institutional vision of community colleges. *Community College Review, 35,* 4.

Aldrich, C. (2003, March). The new core of leadership: In depth interview with leaders across industries reveal essential qualities. *Technology & Development.* Retrieved from http://findarticles.com/p/articles/mi_m0MNT/is_3_57/ai_98901481

Alfred, R. (1998). Redesigning community college to compete for the future. *Community College Journal of Research and Practice, 22*(4), 315-333.

Altbach, P., Berdahl, R., & Gumport, P. J. (1999). *American higher education in the twenty-first century. Social, political, and economic challenges.* Baltimore, MD: The John Hopkins University Press.

American Association of Community Colleges, (2001). *Leadership 2020: Recruitment, preparation, and support.* Washington, DC. Author. (ERICDoucment Reproduction NO. ED 468766

American Association of Community Colleges. (2006). *Competencies for community college leaders. Data Base* Washington, DC: American Association of Community Colleges.

American Association of Community Colleges (2007). *Community College Succession Planning: Preparing the next generation of women for leadership roles.* Retrieved from http://www.docstoc.com/docs/77552627/Community-college-succession-planning-Preparing-the-next-generation-of-women-for-leadership-roles

American Association of Community Colleges. (2008).
Joint Statement on Leadership and Diversity. Data Base
Washington, DC: American Association of Community Colleges

American Association of Community College Trustees (2008).
Joint Statement on Leadership and Diversity. Data Base
Washington, DC: American Association of Community Colleges.

American Psychological Association. (2002). *Publication manual of the*
American Psychological Association. (5th ed.). Washington,
DC: Author.

Amey, M., Jessup-Anger, E., & Jessup-Anger, J. (2008, January 1).
Community college governance: What matters and why? New
directions for community colleges, (ERIC Document Production
Service No. EJ788753). Retrieved from ERIC database.

Amey, M. J., & VanDerLinden, K. E., (2006). *Minorities in higher*
education: Twenty-second annual status reports. Washington, DC. American
Council on Education.

Andrews, A. C. & Fonseci, J. W. (1998). Community colleges in the United States: A
geographical perspective. *Ohio University Press*, 1-7. Retrieved from
http://www.zanesville.ohiou.edu/geography/communitycollege/default.htm.

Avolio, B. J., & Bass, B. M. (2002) *Developing potential across a full range of leadership cases*
on transactional and transformational leadership. Mahwah, NJ: Lawrence Erlbaum
Associates.

Baker, G. A. III., Dudziak., J., & Tyler P. (1994). *A handbook on the community college in America: Its history, mission and management.* Westport, CT: Greenwood Press.

Baker, R. L. (1999) The social work dictionary. (4th ed.). Washington, D. C: National Association of Social Workers Press.

Bennis, W. G. (2000). *Managing the dream: Reflections on Leadership and Change. Cambridge,* MA: Persues Publishing.

Berry, J. W. (1980). Acculturation as varieties of adaptation. In A. M. Padilla (Ed.). *Acculturation: Theory, models and some new findings.* Boulder, Co: Westview.

Bers, T. H., & Calhoun, H. D. (2002). *Next steps for the community college.* San Francisco: Jossey-Bass Publishers.

Betts, K., Urias, D., Chavez, J., & Betts, K. (2009). Higher education and shifting U. S. demographics: Need for visible administrative career paths, professional development, succession planning & commitment to diversity. *Educational Leadership Journal,* 7(2), 1

Boggs, G. R. (2003, Fall). Leadership context for the twenty-first century. New directions for community colleges, (123), 15-25. (ERIC document Reproduction Service No. EJ678130) Retrieved from ERIC database.

Bolman, L. G. & Deal, T. E. (2003). *Reframing organizations: Artistry, choice and leadership.* San Francisco: Jossey-Bass.

Brown, L., Martinez, M., & Daniel D. (2008). Community college leadership preparation: Needs, perceptions, and recommendations. *Community College Review.* 30, 1.

Carlson, B. (2007). *Succession Leadership: Preparing leaders in Colorado community college system.* Ann Arbor: ProQuest.

Cashman, K. (1998). *Leadership from inside out: Becoming a leader for life.* Minneapolis, MN: LeaderSource.

Catana, L. (2005). The concept of system of philosophy. The case of Jacob Bruker's historiography of philosophy. *History and Theory, 44*(1), 72-91.

Chappell, C. (2008). *The new wave of young presidents. Community College Times.* The American Association of Community Colleges. Retrieved from http://www.communitycollegetimes.com/article.cfm?Articled=685.

Chemers, M. (1997). An integrative theory of leadership. Mahwah, NJ: Erlbaum.

Claxton, C. (2007). Placing our assumptions at risk. Pathways to changing the culture of community college. *Community College Journal of Research and Practice.* 32(3), 217-229.

Clunies, J. P. (2004). Benchmarking succession planning and executive development in higher education. *Academic Leadership.* 2, (4).

Cohen, A. M., & Brawer, F. B. (2002). *Next steps for community colleges.* New directions for community colleges. New York: Jossey-Bass.

Community Colleges Leadership Development Initiative (2000). *Meeting new challenges in the community colleges.* Claremont Graduate University, CA. (ERIC Document Reproduction No. ED 447888).

Covey, S. R. (1991). *Principle centered leadership.* New York: Summit.

Creswell, J. (2003). *Research design: Qualitative, quantitative and mixed methods approaches.* Thousand Oaks. CA: Sage.

Creswell, J. W., & Plano Clark, V. L. (2007). *Designing and conducting mixed methods research.* Thousand Oaks. CA: Sage.

Creswell, J. W., &Plano Clark, V. L. (2008). *The Mixed Methods Reader.* Thousand Oaks, CA: Sage

Darwin, A. & Palmer, E. (2009). Mentoring circles in higher education. *Higher Education Research & Development,* 28, (4), 125-136.

Davis, E. B. (2008). Colleges need to offer clear paths to leadership. *The Chronicle of Higher Education* (7), 1-4.
http://chronicle.com.library.edu/article/Colleges-Need-to-Offer-Clea/16225/

Dickey, C. (1996a). The role of quality mentoring in the recruitment and retention of women students of color at the University of Minnesota (Doctoral thesis, University of Minnesota). Retrieved from ERIC database. ED393345.

Dickey, C. (1996b). Mentoring women of color at the University of Minnesota: Challenges for organizational transformation. Retrieved from ERIC database. ED 399838.

Dorsey, M. E. B. (2004). *Leadership development survey responses.* Retrieved from www.ccleadership.org/pdfs/Underserved_Survey.pdf.

Duree, C. (2008). Iowa State Study of community college presidents finds national shortage on horizon. Retrieved from http://www.publiciastate.edu//-mscentra/news/08jul/ccleadershipshtml.

Eddy, P. L. (2009). Wanted: Community-college leaders to serve in the hinterlands. *The Chronicle of Higher Education,* (3), 1-5. Retrieved from http://chronicle.com.library.capella.edu/article/Wanted-Community College-L/33826/

Esters, L. L. & Mosby, D. C. (2007). Disappearing acts: The vanishing black male on community college campuses. *Issues in Higher Education,* 24(14), 1-3.

Evelyn, J. (2001). Community colleges face a crisis of leadership. *The Chronicle of Higher Education,* (4), 1-7.

Firestein, M., (2009). *William Rainey Harper.* Retrieved from http://www.harpercollege.edu/library/archives/williamraineyharper.shtml

Fulton-Calkins, P. & Milling, G. (2005). Community college leadership: An art to be practiced: 2010 and beyond. Community College *Journal of Research and Practice,* 29, 233-250.

Gall, M. D., Gall, J. P., & Borg, W. R. (2003). *Educational research: An introduction.* Boston, Pearson Education.

Gardner, J. W. (1990). *On leadership.* New York: The Free Press.

Gener, R. (2006). One on one, face to face: As mentoring gains fresh currency, new programs inside and outside the academy are redefining the mission and roles. *American Theatre,* 23, 1.

Goldrick, R. S., Harris, D. N., Mazzeo, C. & Kienzl, G. (2009). Transforming America's community colleges: A federal policy proposal to expand opportunity and promote economic prosperity. *Brookings Policy Brief.* Retrieved from http://www.blueprintprosperity.org

Goodchild, L. F. & Wechsler, H. S. (Eds.). (1997). *The history of higher
education. American Association of Higher Education.* Boston: Pearson.

Goode, T. D. (2009) National Center for Cultural Competence.

Gorard, S., & Taylor, C. (2004). *Combining methods in educational
research.* New York: McGraw-Hill.

Gore, T. L. (1995). *Neglected heroes: Leadership and war in the early
medieval period.* Westport, CT: Praeger.

Gould, E. (2007a, April). *Mission survival? Technology and the challenge to the community
college.* Paper presented at the American Association of Community Colleges
Conference, Tampa, Florida.

Gould, E. (2007b, October). Trends and challenges in the community college. Webcast.
Capella University, Minneapolis, Minnesota.

Gould, E. O. & Caldwell, P. F. (1998). Tomorrow's essentials in management; decentralization,
collaboration, and ownership. Community *College Research and Practice Journal*, 22(4),
349-361.
Greenberg, M. (1997). The new GI bill is no match for the original. *Chronicle of
Higher Education.* 54(46) 1. Retrieved from
http://chronicle.comlibrary.capella.edu. ERIC Database. EJ806467

Greenleaf, R. K (1969). *The crisis of leadership: On becoming a servant leader.* San Francisco:
Jossey-Bass.

Greenleaf, R. K. (1970). *The servant leader.* Indianapolis: The Robert Greenleaf Center.

Hopkins, R. A. & Grigoriu, E. (2005). Mentoring community college faculty and staff:

Balancing contradictions of informal program components and formal program structure. *Community College Review,* 32, (4), 1-12.

House, R. J., Hanges, P. J., Javidan, M., Dorfman, P. W., & Gupta, V. (2004). *Culture, leadership, and organizations: The globe study of 62 societies.* Thousand Oaks, CA: Sage.

Hull, J.R. & Keim, M. C. (2007). Nature and status of community college leadership development programs. *Community College Journal of Research and Practice,* 31, 689-702.

Jamilah, E. (n.d). The outsider: From boss to campus leader. *The Chronicle of Higher Educaiton* [wwwpage]. URL at http://chronicle.com/colloquy/2006/03

Johnson, B., & Onwuegbuzie, A. J. (2004). Mixed method research: A research whose time has come. *Educational Researcher.* 33(7), 14-26.

Kezar, A. J., Carducci, R., & McGavin, M. (2006). *Rethinking "L" in higher education leadership. American Association of Higher Education Report.* 31(6), 101-136. Retrieved from ERIC Database EJ791616.

Kotterman, J. (2006). Leadership versus management: What's the difference? *Journal of Quality & Participation,* 29(2), 13-17.

Lancaster, M. (2007) *Succeeding at Succession.* Retrieved from http://www.nccommunitycolleges.edu/external_affairs/president/Sucession Trustees07.htm

League for Innovation in the Community College. (2004, October 19). *What do CEOs want to know about....leadership development?* Quarterly Survey

Leubsdorf, B. (2006). Boomers' retirement may create talent squeeze. *The Chronicle
of Higher Education.* 53(2), 51-51. Retrieved from
Academic Search Premier Database.

Lopez-Molina, G. (2008). *Leadership reconsidered: A mixed methods study of
developing future leaders in the community college.* Retrieved from ProQuest
database. (AAT3315239).

Losco, J. & Fife, B. L. (2000). *Higher education in transition: The challenges of
the new millennium.* Westport, CT: Bergin & Garvey Publishers.

Lynham, S. (2002). The general method of theory-building research in applied disciplines.
Advances in Human Resource Development, 4(3), 221-241.

Mendez-Morse, S. (2004, October). Constructing mentors: Latina educational leader role models
and mentors. Educational Administration Quarterly (40), 4, 561-590.

Michael, C. N., & Young, N. D. (2006). *Preparing the next generation of school
administrators: Advice from veteran leaders.* Retrieved on January
20, 2007 from http://www.eric.ed.gov/ERICDocs/data/ericdocs2/
content storage 01/0000000b/80/32/s6/dc.pdf.

Miller, B. W., Hotes, R. W., & Terry Jr., J. D. (1983). *Leadership in higher
education: A handbook for practicing administrators.* Westport. CT:
Greenwood Press.

Miner, J. B. (2002). *Organizational behavior: Foundations, theories, and
analyses.* New York: Oxford University Press

Molinsky, A. (2007) "Cross-cultural code-switching: the psychological challenges of adapting
behavior in foreign cultural interactions", Academy of Management Review, Vol. 32 No.
2, pp. 622-640.

Morgan, D. L. (2007). Paradigms lost and pragmatism regained: methodological implications of combining qualitative and quantitative methods. *Journal of Mixed Methods Research,* 1, 48.

Moser, P. K., Mulder, D. H., & Trout, J. D. (1998). *The theory of knowledge.* New York: Oxford.

National Center for Cultural Competence. (2009). *Definition of terms.* Retrieved on August 16, 20009at http://www.culturalbroker.info/8_definitions/index.html.

Newman, I., & Benz, C. R. (1998). *Qualitative-quantitative research methodology: Exploring the interactive continuum.* Carbondale, IL: University Press.

Obama. B. (2009) On higher education leadership. Retrieved from http://www. Whitehouse.gov/the press office/Remarks-by-the-President-on-Higher-Education

O'Banion, T. (2006). Crisis and calamity in the community college: Preparing faculty and administrators for the 21st century. *Community College Journal,* 77(3), 44.

Outcalt, C. L. (2002). *Characteristics, practices, challenges: New directions for community colleges.* San Francisco: Jossey-Bass.

Page, O. C. (2003). Promoting diversity in academic leadership. *New Directions for Higher Education,* 124, 79-86.

Park., D. G. Jr. (2006). *The community college leadership crisis and executive research.* American Association of Community Colleges. Washington, DC.

Parkman, A., & Beard R. (2008). *Succession planning and the imposter phenomenon in higher education.* Retrieved from http://jamiesmithportfolio.com/EDTE800/wp-content/Imposter%20Syndrome/Parkman.pdf

Pattenaude, R. L. (2002). Administering the modern university: In Brian L. Fife,
& J. Losco (EDS.). *Higher education in transition: The challenges of the
new millennium,* (p. 159). Westport, CT: Bergin & Garvey.

Pedersen, R. T. (1997) Value conflict on the Community College Campus: An examination of its
historical origin. In Goodchild, L. F. & Wechsler, H. S (Eds.). The history of higher
education (499-509). Boston, MA: Pearson.

Peterson, M. W., Dill, D. D., & Mets, L. A. (1997). *A handbook on redesigning
Post-secondary institutions: Planning and management for a changing
environment.* San Francisco: Jossey-Bass.

Polleys, M. S. (2002). One university's response to the anti-leadership vaccine: Developing
servant leaders. *Journal of Leadership Studies,* (8), 14.

Ramsden, P. (2000). *Learning to lead in higher education.* New York:
RoutledgeFalmer.

Rendon, L. (2003). *Educating the largest minority group. Chronicle of Higher Education.*
Retrieved from
http://chronicle.com.library.capella.edu/article/Educating-the-Largest-Minor/26097/

Reyes, M., & Halcon, J. J. (1998). Racism in academia: the old wolf revisited.
Harvard Education Review, 58(3), 299-314.

Rosenbach, W. E. & Taylor, R. (1998). Contemporary issues in leadership.
Boulder, Co: Westview Press.

Ruse, D., & Janeen, K. (2008). *Using human capital planning to predict the future talent
needs: Planning organization effectiveness.* CUPA-HR (1), 28-23.

Sashkin, M. S., & Sashkin, M. G. (2002). *Leadership that matters: The critical factors for making a difference in people's lives in organizations' success.* London: Barrett-Koehler.

Senge, P. M. (1990). *The fifth discipline.* New York: Doubleday.

Shults, C. (2001). *The critical impact of impending retirements on community college leadership.* American Association of Community Colleges. Washington, DC. (ERIC Document Reproduction NO. ED. 451833.

Stembert, R., Antonakis, J., & Cianciolo, A. (2004). *The nature of leadership.* London: Sage.

Story, J. (2004). *Leadership in organizations: Current issues and key trends.* New York: RoutledgeFalmer.

Succession Planning. (2009). In American heritage dictionary of the English language (4th ed., p. 592). Boston, MA: Houghton Mifflin.

Szenlenyi, K. (2001). *Minority student retention and academic achievement in community colleges. ERIC Digest.* Retrieved on August 22, 2009 at hhtp://www.ericdigests.org/2001-4/minority.html.

Towsend, B. K., & Twombly, S. B. (2001). *Community colleges: Policy in the future context.* Wesptort, CT: Ablex

Tropiano, Jr., M. (May/June 2004). Effective succession planning. *Organizational Development,* 50-53.

Valeau, E. J. & Boggs, G. R. (2004). An assessment of the Association of California Community

College mentor program. *Community College Review*, 31(4), 1-9, Retrieved from Academic
Search Premier Database.

Valverde, L. A. (2003). *Leaders of color in higher education: Unrecognized
triumphs in harsh institutions*. Walnut Creek, CA: Alta Mira Press.

Varney, J. (2009). Humanistic mentoring: Nurturing the person within. *Kappa Delta Pi Record*,
45 (3), 127-131.

Vaughn, G. (2000). *The community college story*. Washington, DC. Community
College Press.

Viniar, B. (2006). *From boss to campus leader*. Retrieved from http://chroncile.com/colloquy.

Viniar, B. (2008). *Community college researchers examine leadership competencies*. Institute for
Community College Development. Retrieved from
http://www.iccd.cornell.edu/iccd/news/enews/spring08_leadershipComp.html

Walker, D. E. (1979). *The effective administrator*. San Francisco: Jossey-Bass.

Wallin, D., Cameron, D. W., & Sharples, K. (2005). Succession planning and
targeted leadership development. *Community College Journal*,
76(1), 19-24.

Watts, G. E. (2002). *Enhancing community college through professional
development: New directions for community colleges*. Little Rock,
Arkansas: Jossey-Bass.

Weisman, I., & Vaughan, G. (2006). A profile of community-college presidents. *The Chronicle
of Higher Education*. (10), 27

Wheeler, D. L. (2007). 10 tips for aspiring community college presidents. *The Chronicle of Higher Education*, 53, 34 (EJ763843).

Wolverton, M. (1999). Task-Based Information Management. *In ACM Computing Surveys (CSUR)*, vol. 32. No 10. ACM Press.

Wolverton, M. Gmelch, W. H., Wolverton, M. L., & Sarros, J. C. (1999). Stress in academic leadership: U. S. and Australian department chairs/heads. *The Review of Higher Education*, 22(2), 165-185.

Yukl, G. (1989). Managerial leadership: A review of theory and research. *Journal of Management*, 15(2), 251-289.

APPENDIX A. DEMOGRAPHICS AND SUCCESSION PLANNING SURVEY FOR PARTICIPANTS AT SELECTED NORTH CAROLINA COMMUNITY COLLEGE

Note. From Leadership Reconsidered: A Mixed Methods Study of Developing Future Leaders in the Community College (p. 110), by Generosa Lopez-Molina, 2008. Doctoral dissertation, Capella University, Minnesota. Retrieved April 5, 2009, from Dissertations & Theses: Full Text database. (Publication No. AAT 3315239) (Adapted with permission.)

Introduction to the Survey

Your willingness to participate in this important succession planning research study is appreciated. Succession planning is the "process of identifying and preparing a suitable employee for apposition or replacement of an employee in a different role within the organization or institution through job rotation, training and mentoring," according to Lopez-Molina (2008).

Your responses to this survey are confidential. As outlined in the consent form my dissertation research title is: Community College Leadership Crisis: Identifying and Preparing Future Leaders through Succession Planning in Select North Carolina Community Colleges.

This two-part survey will collect demographical data, and collect information relevant to leadership development and succession planning practices of selected community colleges. The second part of the data gathering will consist of an interview conducted via telephone or in-person. The interview will be audiotape recorded on cassettes. I will follow-up with you for scheduling the interview after you have completed the survey. Individuals participating in both parts of the study will receive a copy of the research findings upon request. As a reminder, the names of participants and institutions will be kept confidential and will be coded in the research findings report. This survey will take approximately 15-20 minutes to complete. I thank you so very much for completing this survey in a timely manner.

Let's begin.

Part One: Demographical Data for Senior Administrative Participant

1. Please answer the following questions:

   Name

   Institution

   Title

   Telephone Number

   City/Town

   State/Province

   Zip/Postal Code

   Country

2. How many years have you served in this role? _____

3. What are the demographics of the service area of the community college? (Statistical characteristics of human population such as gender, race ethnicity.)

   Total Population

   Gender: Male/Female

   Age Distribution

   Race & Ethnicity:

   White

   Black or African American

   American Indian or Alaska Native

   Asian

   Native Hawaiian or Other Pacific Islander

   Hispanic/Latino (For example, Cuban, Mexican, Puerto Rican.)

   Other Race

4. What is the total number of employees at the community college? Include full-time faculty, staff and administration, and part-time staff and adjunct faculty, and ethnicity of each employee classification.

Total Employees

Total Full-Time Faculty

____Full-Time Staff

____Full-Time Professional/Technical

____Full-Time Administration

Total Part-Time Employees

____Part-Time Adjunct Faculty

____Part-Time Staff

____Part-Time Professional/Technical

____Part-Time Administration

5. How many of the following academic administrators are employed at your institution in the following categories: (Identify ethnicity in each category.)

President

Executive Vice President

Vice President

Dean

Chair

6. How many of the following classified administrators are potential retirees based on retirement eligibility at your institution in the following categories: (Identify ethnicity in each category.)

President

Executive Vice President

Vice President

Dean

Chair

Part Two: Developing Future Leaders

(Individuals currently preparing themselves to lead organizations or institutions.)

7. Upon hiring new employees, does the community college offer pathways for upward mobility within and across classification? (pathways in succession planning to senior level positions through formal and informal mentoring programs.)

    ☐ Yes

    ☐ No

8. If your answer to question number 8 is Yes, please explain the process upon hiring.

9. If your answer to number 8 is No, please explain why not.

10. Does the community college provide professional development programs or activities for individuals aspiring to assume leadership roles such as president or vice president? (Professional development: specific and strategic building or expanding on the knowledge, skills, and abilities for effective leadership with desired outcomes and expectations.)

    ☐ Yes

    ☐ No

11. If your answer to question 11 is Yes, list the professional development programs or activities offered and their frequency.

    Program_____ Frequency_____

    Program_____ Frequency_____

    Program_____ Frequency_____

    Program_____ Frequency_____

    Program_____ Frequency_____

12. If your answer to number 11 is No, please explain why not.

13. Does the college provide a mentoring program for new employees?
    ☐ Yes
    ☐ No

14. If your answer to number 14 is Yes, is the mentoring formal or informal?
    ☐ Formal
    ☐ Informal

15. If you answer to number 14 is Yes, please describe the mentoring program.

16. If your answer to question 14 is No, why not? Please explain.

17. Is there a succession plan for administrators at your community college?
    (Succession plan: identifying and preparing a suitable employee for a position
    or replacement of an employee in different role within the organization or
    institution through job rotation, training and mentoring e. g. individuals aspiring
    to lead organizations or institutions.
    ☐ Yes
    ☐ No

18. If your answer to number 18 is Yes, how are individuals identified and selected to
    participate in succession planning processes?

19. If your answer to question 18 is Yes, please discuss the employee classifications
    that participate in succession planning programs.

20. If your answer to question number 18 is No, why not? Please explain.

21. Are your succession planning programs related to the leadership development
    program at your institution? Please explain the relationship.

22. What strategies in succession planning related to leadership development programs are used to include individuals from minority populations? Please discuss in as much detail as possible.

23. How many of the current senior leaders are graduates of succession planning programs at your institution? (Senior leaders such as President, Executive vice President, Vice President, and Dean.)

24. How many of the current senior leaders have completed professional development programs and became leaders at your institution?

25. How many of the current senior leaders have participated in any leadership development program? Please indicate how many, and identify the name/s of the leadership development programs.

26. How are future leaders identified and selected at your institution to participate in leadership development and succession planning processes? (Future leaders: Individuals currently preparing themselves to lead organizations or institutions.) Identified Selected

27. In concluding the survey, is there anything else you would like to share that would be valuable information to the research study?

28. Will you be participating with the follow-up telephone interview or in-person interview?
(Please check the appropriate box.)
☐ Telephone Interview
☐ In-person Interview

This concludes the two-part survey. Thank you for your participation. The researcher will be communicating with you to invite you to schedule a fifteen minute telephone or in-person interview.

APPENDIX. B

Note. From Leadership Reconsidered: A Mixed Methods Study of Developing Future Leaders in the Community College (p. 117), by Generosa Lopez-Molina, 2008. Doctoral dissertation, Capella University, Minnesota. Retrieved April 5, 2009, from Dissertations & Theses: Full Text database. (Publication No. AAT 3315239) (Adapted with permission.)

FOLLOW-UP QUESTIONS INTERVIEW (SCRIPT)

Your willingness to participate in this follow-up interview is most appreciated. To reiterate, the research study title is: Community College Leadership Crisis: Identifying and Preparing Future Leaders through Succession Planning in Select North Carolina Community Colleges. You have completed the two-part survey consisting of demographical data and information relevant to succession planning for leadership development and succession planning practices at select North Carolina community colleges.

This follow-up interview is being audiotape recorded on cassettes. This interview should take approximately 15 minutes. By participating in this part of the study, you will receive a copy of the research findings, upon request.

Please remember that the names of the participants and institutions will remain confidential and research materials will be coded in this research findings report.

Do you have any questions for me before we begin?

Questions:

1. What would you consider to be the strengths and challenges of your current leadership development programming efforts?

2. What would you consider to be the strengths and challenges to the existing mentoring efforts at the college?

3. Are the strengths and challenges the same with the minority candidates? If not, how are they different?

    a. How are cultural nuances addressed when mentoring minority candidates?

    b. What topics do you foresee needing further study in developing leaders of the minority populations?

This concludes our interview. I thank you for your participation.

Printed in the United States
By Bookmasters